Topical
Spanish
Review
Grammar

TOPICAL
Spanish Review Grammar

R. L. Predmore
Duke University

HENRY HOLT & COMPANY
New York

To

E. W. Billetdoux

Preface

This is a brief review of the essentials of Spanish grammar. It was written for those teachers who consider it necessary to review in the second year the fundamentals of grammar but who wish to do it in such a way as to save a maximum of time for conversation and reading based on materials of their own choosing.

A few grammatical points often treated in review grammars have been eliminated from this one, because to teach them adequately consumes more class time than is warranted by the gain to second-year students. This book does nothing, for instance, to encourage the discussion of such points as the use of articles in appositional phrases. (Should the student say, "Madrid, capital de España" or "Madrid, la capital de España"?) Some other points deliberately omitted are the complex agreement of adjectives, the multiple possibilities of relatives, all conceivable combinations of tense and mood in conditional sentences. The brevity of this book is not due, however, to these omissions but rather to the elimination of readings, conversations, and the like. The fundamentals of Spanish grammar are here treated at least as fully as in most books of its kind.

The grammar is presented topically. Wherever possible, the chapters have been limited to one major topic per chapter. Where this has not been possible, the entire topic has been presented in consecutive chapters, so that in no case need the student skip from chapter to chapter to appendix in order to piece together the full treatment of a given point. There is nothing sacrosanct about the order in which the topics are presented. The author believes, nevertheless, that the verb deserves to come first. Many books allow the uses of the subjunctive, for example, to get lost in the feeble fag-end of the semester. Here the subjunctive is given a fair chance to survive.

The book is designed to be flexible in use. The order of the chapters can be altered, the number of weeks devoted to grammar review can be increased or reduced. For those who like to do some grammar in each class period, the review can be accomplished in about twelve weeks by using twenty minutes of class time per hour, three times a week. For those who prefer to concentrate the review into half a semester or less, the book can be taken at the rate of two chapters per period.

In choosing the materials to be treated in this review the author has been guided in large part by Hayward Keniston's *Spanish Syntax List* and his *A Standard List of Spanish Words and Idioms*.

For helpful suggestions calculated to perfect the Spanish examples presented in this book the author gratefully acknowledges his debt to Professor Elías Torre.

R. L. PREDMORE

Jan. 1, 1954   Durham, N. C.

Contents

1. REGULAR VERBS . . . .

PRESENT INDICATIVE	PRESENT SUBJUNCTIVE	IMPERFECT INDICATIVE	FUTURE INDICATIVE

1ST CONJUGATION: comprar, *to buy* . . . .

I buy, do buy, am buying, etc.	*(that) I may buy, etc.*	*I was buying, used to buy, etc.*	*I will buy, etc.*
compro	compre	compraba	compraré
compras	compres	comprabas	comprarás
compra	compre	compraba	comprará
compramos	compremos	comprábamos	compraremos
compráis	compréis	comprabais	compraréis
compran	compren	compraban	comprarán

2ND CONJUGATION: comer, *to eat* . . . .

I eat, do eat, am eating, etc.	*(that) I may eat, etc.*	*I was eating, used to eat, etc.*	*I will eat, etc.*
como	coma	comía	comeré
comes	comas	comías	comerás
come	coma	comía	comerá
comemos	comamos	comíamos	comeremos
coméis	comáis	comíais	comeréis
comen	coman	comían	comerán

3RD CONJUGATION: recibir, *to receive* . . . .

I receive, do receive, am receiving, etc.	*(that) I may receive, etc.*	*I was receiving, used to receive, etc.*	*I will receive, etc.*
recibo	reciba	recibía	recibiré
recibes	recibas	recibías	recibirás
recibe	reciba	recibía	recibirá
recibimos	recibamos	recibíamos	recibiremos
recibís	recibáis	recibíais	recibiréis
reciben	reciban	recibían	recibirán

GRAMMAR

A. Study the forms and meanings given above.

B. Memorize the meanings, and learn the simple tenses of these verbs:

ganar, to win, earn	**comprender,** to under-	**asistir,** to attend (be
llamar, to call, name	stand	present)
mirar, to look (at)	**correr,** to run	**decidir,** to decide
preguntar, to ask	**responder,** to reply	**partir,** to divide; to depart
(*a question*)	**temer,** to fear	**permitir,** to permit
trabajar, to work	**vender,** to sell	**subir,** to climb, go up

[2]

CONDITIONAL INDICATIVE	PRETERITE INDICATIVE	IMPERFECT SUBJUNCTIVE 1	IMPERFECT SUBJUNCTIVE 2 *
. . . . −**ar** VERBS			
I would buy, etc.	*I bought, etc.*	*(that) I might buy, etc.*	*(that) I might buy, etc.*
compraría	compré	comprara	comprase
comprarías	compraste	compraras	comprases
compraría	compró	comprara	comprase
compraríamos	compramos	compráramos	comprásemos
compraríais	comprasteis	comprarais	compraseis
comprarían	compraron	compraran	comprasen
. . . . −**er** VERBS			
I would eat, etc.	*I ate, etc.*	*(that) I might eat, etc.*	*(that) I might eat, etc.*
comería	comí	comiera	comiese
comerías	comiste	comieras	comieses
comería	comió	comiera	comiese
comeríamos	comimos	comiéramos	comiésemos
comeríais	comisteis	comierais	comieseis
comerían	comieron	comieran	comiesen
. . . . −**ir** VERBS			
I would receive, etc.	*I received, etc.*	*(that) I might receive, etc.*	*(that) I might receive, etc.*
recibiría	recibí	recibiera	recibiese
recibirías	recibiste	recibieras	recibieses
recibiría	recibió	recibiera	recibiese
recibiríamos	recibimos	recibiéramos	recibiésemos
recibiríais	recibisteis	recibierais	recibieseis
recibirían	recibieron	recibieran	recibiesen

* The imperfect subjunctive has two sets of endings. The forms in −**ra** are the more common ones.

EXERCISES

The exercises of the first seven chapters of this book are intended for drill on forms, not uses. Therefore, when the English does not clearly identify the desired tense, it is indicated.

A. Translate, using the proper forms of the simple indicative tenses: 1. We sell, ask, receive. 2. They call, decide, fear. 3. You (*fam.*

sing.) look, run, attend. 4. We were working, eating, departing. 5. I bought, understood, climbed (*pret.*). 6. He would earn, reply, permit (*cond.*). 7. They called, understood, decided (*pret.*). 8. We shall look, eat, depart. 9. I was climbing, running, asking. 10. You (*fam. pl.*) will sell, receive, earn. 11. We feared, permitted, worked (*pret.*). 12. He was earning, receiving, running.

B. Translate, using the correct forms of the present subjunctive: **Ella se alegra de que:** 1. I receive, sell, work. 2. He buys, understands, attends. 3. We eat, look, depart.

C. Translate, using the correct forms of the imperfect subjunctive: **Ella se alegraba de que:** 1. They looked, replied, climbed. 2. I called, decided, feared. 3. We sold, permitted, earned.

2. REGULAR VERBS . . . .

PRESENT PERFECT INDICATIVE	PLUPERFECT INDICATIVE *	FUTURE PERFECT INDICATIVE
I have bought, etc.	*I had bought, etc.*	*I will have bought, etc.*
he comprado	había comprado	habré comprado
has comprado	habías comprado	habrás comprado
ha comprado	había comprado	habrá comprado
hemos comprado	habíamos comprado	habremos comprado
habéis comprado	habíais comprado	habréis comprado
han comprado	habían comprado	habrán comprado

* In Spanish there is also a preterite perfect tense composed of the preterite of haber (**hube, hubiste, hubo, hubimos, hubisteis, hubieron**) and the past participle. It is the least frequent of all the Spanish tenses and need not be learned for active use. It may be translated just like the pluperfect.

GRAMMAR

A. The compound tenses are composed of the proper form of the auxiliary **haber** and the past participle of the verb.

B. Regular past participles are formed by adding –**ado** to the stem of –**ar** verbs, and –**ido** to the stems of –**er** and –**ir** verbs: **comprado, comido, recibido.** REMEMBER: The past participle always ends in –o when used with **haber.**

C. The proper form of **haber** may be combined with any past participle to form the desired compound tense of the verb whose past participle is used. Learn the following irregular participles:

abrir: **abierto**, opened
cubrir: **cubierto**, covered
decir: **dicho**, said
escribir: **escrito**, written

hacer: **hecho**, done
morir: **muerto**, died
poner: **puesto**, put

romper: **roto**, broken
ver: **visto**, seen
volver: **vuelto**, returned

[6]

...... COMPOUND TENSES

CONDITIONAL PERF. INDICATIVE	PRESENT PERFECT SUBJUNCTIVE	PLUPERFECT SUBJUNCTIVE *
I would have bought, etc.	*(that) I may have bought, etc.*	*(that) I might have bought, etc.*
habría comprado	haya comprado	hubiera comprado
habrías comprado	hayas comprado	hubieras comprado
habría comprado	haya comprado	hubiera comprado
habríamos comprado	hayamos comprado	hubiéramos comprado
habríais comprado	hayáis comprado	hubierais comprado
habrían comprado	hayan comprado	hubieran comprado

* The pluperfect subjunctive may also be formed with: **hubiese, hubieses, hubiese, hubiésemos, hubieseis, hubiesen.**

EXERCISES

A. *Translate using the correct forms of the compound indicative tenses:*
1. I have written, eaten, spoken. 2. He had done, earned, decided.
3. We have put, returned, departed. 4. We will have seen, said, looked. 5. They have feared, received, opened. 6. You (*fam. sing.*) would have covered, seen, broken.

B. *Translate using the correct forms of the present perfect subjunctive:*
Él siente que: 1. They have sold, worked, died. 2. We have opened, put, spoken. 3. I have said, done, looked. 4. You (*fam. pl.*) have departed, returned, written.

C. *Translate using the correct forms of the pluperfect subjunctive:*
Él sentía que: 1. We had covered, eaten, received. 2. She had sold, earned, seen. 3. They had feared, returned, said.

3. IRREGULAR VERBS . . . .

INFINITIVE & PARTICIPLES	PRESENT INDICATIVE	PRESENT SUBJUNCTIVE	IMPERFECT INDICATIVE	FUTURE INDICATIVE
1. andar to walk andando andado	ando andas anda andamos andáis andan	ande andes ande andemos andéis anden	andaba andabas andaba andábamos andabais andaban	andaré andarás andará andaremos andaréis andarán
2. caber to be contained, fit into cabiendo cabido	quepo cabes cabe cabemos cabéis caben	quepa quepas quepa quepamos quepáis quepan	cabía cabías cabía cabíamos cabíais cabían	cabré cabrás cabrá cabremos cabréis cabrán
3. decir to say, tell diciendo dicho	digo dices dice decimos decís dicen	diga digas diga digamos digáis digan	decía decías decía decíamos decíais decían	diré dirás dirá diremos diréis dirán
4. estar to be estando estado	estoy estás está estamos estáis están	esté estés esté estemos estéis estén	estaba estabas estaba estábamos estabais estaban	estaré estarás estará estaremos estaréis estarán
5. haber to have habiendo habido	he has ha hemos habéis han	haya hayas haya hayamos hayáis hayan	había habías había habíamos habíais habían	habré habrás habrá habremos habréis habrán
6. hacer to make, do haciendo hecho	hago haces hace hacemos hacéis hacen	haga hagas haga hagamos hagáis hagan	hacía hacías hacía hacíamos hacíais hacían	haré harás hará haremos haréis harán
7. poder to be able, can pudiendo podido	puedo puedes puede podemos podéis pueden	pueda puedas pueda podamos podáis puedan	podía podías podía podíamos podíais podían	podré podrás podrá podremos podréis podrán

[8]

CONDITIONAL	PRETERITE INDICATIVE	I. IMPERFECT SUBJUNCTIVE	II. IMPERFECT SUBJUNCTIVE	IMPERA- TIVE
andaría	anduve	anduviera	anduviese	
andarías	anduviste	anduvieras	anduvieses	anda
andaría	anduvo	anduviera	anduviese	
andaríamos	anduvimos	anduviéramos	anduviésemos	
andaríais	anduvisteis	anduvierais	anduvieseis	andad
andarían	anduvieron	anduvieran	anduviesen	
cabría	cupe	cupiera	cupiese	
cabrías	cupiste	cupieras	cupieses	cabe
cabría	cupo	cupiera	cupiese	
cabríamos	cupimos	cupiéramos	cupiésemos	
cabrías	cupisteis	cupierais	cupieseis	cabed
cabrían	cupieron	cupieran	cupiesen	
diría	dije	dijera	dijese	
dirías	dijiste	dijeras	dijeses	di
diría	dijo	dijera	dijese	
diríamos	dijimos	dijéramos	dijésemos	
diríais	dijisteis	dijerais	dijeseis	decid
dirían	dijeron	dijeran	dijesen	
estaría	estuve	estuviera	estuviese	
estarías	estuviste	estuvieras	estuvieses	está
estaría	estuvo	estuviera	estuviese	
estaríamos	estuvimos	estuviéramos	estuviésemos	
estaríais	estuvisteis	estuvierais	estuvieseis	estad
estarían	estuvieron	estuvieran	estuviesen	
habría	hube	hubiera	hubiese	
habrías	hubiste	hubieras	hubieses	he
habría	hubo	hubiera	hubiese	
habríamos	hubimos	hubiéramos	hubiésemos	
habríais	hubisteis	hubierais	hubieseis	habed
habrían	hubieron	hubieran	hubiesen	
haría	hice	hiciera	hiciese	
harías	hiciste	hicieras	hicieses	haz
haría	hizo	hiciera	hiciese	
haríamos	hicimos	hiciéramos	hiciésemos	
haríais	hicisteis	hicierais	hicieseis	haced
harían	hicieron	hicieran	hiciesen	
podría	pude	pudiera	pudiese	
podrías	pudiste	pudieras	pudieses	
podría	pudo	pudiera	pudiese	
podríamos	pudimos	pudiéramos	pudiésemos	
podríais	pudisteis	pudierais	pudieseis	
podrían	pudieron	pudieran	pudiesen	

INFINITIVE & PARTICIPLES	PRESENT INDICATIVE	PRESENT SUBJUNCTIVE	IMPERFECT INDICATIVE	FUTURE INDICATIVE
8. poner *to put*	pongo	ponga	ponía	pondré
	pones	pongas	ponías	pondrás
	pone	ponga	ponía	pondrá
poniendo	ponemos	pongamos	poníamos	pondremos
	ponéis	pongáis	poníais	pondréis
puesto	ponen	pongan	ponían	pondrán
9. querer *to want*	quiero	quiera	quería	querré
	quieres	quieras	querías	querrás
	quiere	quiera	quería	querrá
queriendo	queremos	queramos	queríamos	querremos
	queréis	queráis	queríais	querréis
querido	quieren	quieran	querían	querrán
10. saber *to know*	sé	sepa	sabía	sabré
	sabes	sepas	sabías	sabrás
	sabe	sepa	sabía	sabrá
sabiendo	sabemos	sepamos	sabíamos	sabremos
	sabéis	sepáis	sabíais	sabréis
sabido	saben	sepan	sabían	sabrán
11. tener *to have*	tengo	tenga	tenía	tendré
	tienes	tengas	tenías	tendrás
	tiene	tenga	tenía	tendrá
teniendo	tenemos	tengamos	teníamos	tendremos
	tenéis	tengáis	teníais	tendréis
tenido	tienen	tengan	tenían	tendrán
12. venir *to come*	vengo	venga	venía	vendré
	vienes	vengas	venías	vendrás
	viene	venga	venía	vendrá
viniendo	venimos	vengamos	veníamos	vendremos
	venís	vengáis	veníais	vendréis
venido	vienen	vengan	venían	vendrán

A. *Study the forms of the irregular verbs given in this chapter.*

B. Note that the present subjunctive of all these verbs (except **estar, haber, saber**) can be derived from the first person singular of the present indicative. EXAMPLE: **hago: haga.**

C. Note that all of these verbs (except **decir**) have identical preterite endings: **–e, –iste, –o, –imos, –isteis, –ieron.**

D. Note that the imperfect subjunctive of these verbs can be derived from the 3rd pers. pl., pret.: **pudieron: pudiera, pudiese.**

EXERCISES

A. *Change the following forms to the present indicative and to the future:*
1. Anduvimos. 2. Vine. 3. Tuvo. 4. Cupieron. 5. Dijiste.

CONDITIONAL	PRETERITE INDICATIVE	I. IMPERFECT SUBJUNCTIVE	II. IMPERFECT SUBJUNCTIVE	IMPERATIVE
pondría	puse	pusiera	pusiese	
pondrías	pusiste	pusieras	pusieses	pon
pondría	puso	pusiera	pusiese	
pondríamos	pusimos	pusiéramos	pusiésemos	
pondríais	pusisteis	pusierais	pusieseis	poned
pondrían	pusieron	pusieran	pusiesen	
querría	quise	quisiera	quisiese	
querrías	quisiste	quisieras	quisieses	quiere
querría	quiso	quisiera	quisiese	
querríamos	quisimos	quisiéramos	quisiésemos	
querríais	quisisteis	quisierais	quisieseis	quered
querrían	quisieron	quisieran	quisiesen	
sabría	supe	supiera	supiese	
sabrías	supiste	supieras	supieses	sabe
sabría	supo	supiera	supiese	
sabríamos	supimos	supiéramos	supiésemos	
sabríais	supisteis	supierais	supieseis	sabed
sabrían	supieron	supieran	supiesen	
tendría	tuve	tuviera	tuviese	
tendrías	tuviste	tuvieras	tuvieses	ten
tendría	tuvo	tuviera	tuviese	
tendríamos	tuvimos	tuviéramos	tuviésemos	
tendríais	tuvisteis	tuvierais	tuvieseis	tened
tendrían	tuvieron	tuvieran	tuviesen	
vendría	vine	viniera	viniese	
vendrías	viniste	vinieras	vinieses	ven
vendría	vino	viniera	viniese	
vendríamos	vinimos	viniéramos	viniésemos	
vendríais	vinisteis	vinierais	vinieseis	venid
vendrían	vinieron	vinieran	viniesen	

6. Estuvimos. 7. Hubo. 8. Supo. 9. Hice. 10. Pudieron. 11. Pusiste. 12. Quisimos.

B. *Translate:* 1. They walked (*pret.*). 2. I have put. 3. I fit. 4. We came (*pret.*). 5. We shall do. 6. They were saying. 7. She would be (*cond.*). 8. I shall say. 9. He placed (*pret.*). 10. They have. 11. I know. 12. She was able (*pret.*). 13. We wished (*pret.*). 14. I have. 15. They are coming. 16. You (*fam. sing.*) want. 17. They were (*pret.*). 18. We have said. 19. He did (*pret.*).

C. *Translate, using the correct forms of the subjunctive:* **Siento que:** 1. He knows. 2. It doesn't fit. 3. She was able. 4. We did. 5. They say. 6. He has placed. 7. You (*fam. sing.*) were. 8. They come.

D. *Give the familiar imperatives of* **decir, hacer, poner, tener, venir.**

[11]

4. IRREGULAR VERBS • • • • • •

INFINITIVE & PARTICIPLES	PRESENT INDICATIVE	PRESENT SUBJUNCTIVE	IMPERFECT INDICATIVE	FUTURE INDICATIVE
1. caer *to fall* cayendo caído	caigo caes cae caemos caéis caen	caiga caigas caiga caigamos caigáis caigan	caía caías caía caíamos caíais caían	caeré caerás caerá caeremos caeréis caerán
2. conducir *to lead* *conduct* conduciendo conducido	conduzco conduces conduce conducimos conducís conducen	conduzca conduzcas conduzca conduzcamos conduzcáis conduzcan	conducía conducías conducía conducíamos conducíais conducían	conduciré conducirás conducirá conduciremos conduciréis conducirán
3. dar *to give* dando dado	doy das da damos dais dan	dé des dé demos deis den	daba dabas daba dábamos dabais daban	daré darás dará daremos daréis darán
4. ir *to go* yendo ido	voy vas va vamos vais van	vaya vayas vaya vayamos vayáis vayan	iba ibas iba íbamos ibais iban	iré irás irá iremos iréis irán
5. oír *to hear* oyendo oído	oigo oyes oye oímos oís oyen	oiga oigas oiga oigamos oigáis oigan	oía oías oía oíamos oíais oían	oiré oirás oirá oiremos oiréis oirán
6. salir *to go out,* *leave* saliendo salido	salgo sales sale salimos salís salen	salga salgas salga salgamos salgáis salgan	salía salías salía salíamos salíais salían	saldré saldrás saldrá saldremos saldréis saldrán
7. ser *to be* siendo sido	soy eres es somos sois son	sea seas sea seamos seáis sean	era eras era éramos erais eran	seré serás será seremos seréis serán

CONDITIONAL	PRETERITE INDICATIVE	I. IMPERFECT SUBJUNCTIVE	II. IMPERFECT SUBJUNCTIVE	IMPERA- TIVE
caería	caí	cayera	cayese	
caerías	caíste	cayeras	cayeses	cae
caería	cayó	cayera	cayese	
caeríamos	caímos	cayéramos	cayésemos	
caeríais	caísteis	cayerais	cayeseis	caed
caerían	cayeron	cayeran	cayesen	
conduciría	conduje	condujera	condujese	
conducirías	condujiste	condujeras	condujeses	conduce
conduciría	condujo	condujera	condujese	
conduciríamos	condujimos	condujéramos	condujésemos	
conduciríais	condujisteis	condujerais	condujeseis	conducid
conducirían	condujeron	condujeran	condujesen	
daría	di	diera	diese	
darías	diste	dieras	dieses	da
daría	dió	diera	diese	
daríamos	dimos	diéramos	diésemos	
daríais	disteis	dierais	dieseis	dad
darían	dieron	dieran	diesen	
iría	fuí	fuera	fuese	
irías	fuiste	fueras	fueses	ve
iría	fué	fuera	fuese	
iríamos	fuimos	fuéramos	fuésemos	
iríais	fuisteis	fuerais	fueseis	id
irían	fueron	fueran	fuesen	
oiría	oí	oyera	oyese	
oirías	oíste	oyeras	oyeses	oye
oiría	oyó	oyera	oyese	
oiríamos	oímos	oyéramos	oyésemos	
oiríais	oísteis	oyerais	oyeseis	oíd
oirían	oyeron	oyeran	oyesen	
saldría	salí	saliera	saliese	
saldrías	saliste	salieras	salieses	sal
saldría	salió	saliera	saliese	
saldríamos	salimos	saliéramos	saliésemos	
salríais	salisteis	salierais	salieseis	salid
saldrían	salieron	salieran	saliesen	
sería	fuí	fuera	fuese	
serías	fuiste	fueras	fueses	sé
sería	fué	fuera	fuese	
seríamos	fuimos	fuéramos	fuésemos	
seríais	fuisteis	fuerais	fueseis	sed
serían	fueron	fueran	fuesen	

INFINITIVE & PARTICIPLES	PRESENT INDICATIVE	PRESENT SUBJUNCTIVE	IMPERFECT INDICATIVE	FUTURE INDICATIVE
8. traer	traigo	traiga	traía	traeré
to bring	traes	traigas	traías	traerás
	trae	traiga	traía	traerá
trayendo	traemos	traigamos	traíamos	traeremos
	traéis	traigáis	traíais	traeréis
traído	traen	traigan	traían	traerán
9. valer	valgo	valga	valía	valdré
to be	vales	valgas	valías	valdrás
worth	vale	valga	valía	valdrá
valiendo	valemos	valgamos	valíamos	valdremos
	valéis	valgáis	valíais	valdréis
valido	valen	valgan	valían	valdrán
10. ver	veo	vea	veía	veré
to see	ves	veas	veías	verás
	ve	vea	veía	verá
viendo	vemos	veamos	veíamos	veremos
	veis	veáis	veíais	veréis
visto	ven	vean	veían	verán

GRAMMAR

A. *Study the forms of the ten irregular verbs given in this chapter.*

B. Note that the present subjunctive of these verbs (except **dar, ser, ir**) can be derived from the first person singular of the present indicative. EXAMPLE: **oigo: oiga.**

C. Note that the only verbs irregular in the imperfect indicative are: **ir, ser, ver.**

D. Note that the imperfect subjunctive of all of these verbs can be derived from the third person plural of the preterite. EXAMPLE: **dieron: diera, diese.**

E. Note that the preterite and imperfect subjunctive of **ir** and **ser** are identical.

EXERCISES

A. *Change the following forms to the present indicative and to the preterite:* 1. Traerán. 2. Daré. 3. Valdrán. 4. Conducirá. 5. Iremos. 6. Oiré. 7. Caerá. 8. Seremos. 9. Verá. 10. Saldré.

CONDITIONAL	PRETERITE INDICATIVE	I. IMPERFECT SUBJUNCTIVE	II. IMPERFECT SUBJUNCTIVE	IMPERA-TIVE
traería	traje	trajera	trajese	
traerías	trajiste	trajeras	trajeses	trae
traería	trajo	trajera	trajese	
traeríamos	trajimos	trajéramos	trajésemos	
traeríais	trajisteis	trajerais	trajeseis	traed
traerían	trajeron	trajeran	trajesen	
valdría	valí	valiera	valiese	
valdrías	valiste	valieras	valieses	val (vale)
valdría	valió	valiera	valiese	
valdríamos	valimos	valiéramos	valiésemos	
valdríais	valisteis	valierais	valieseis	valed
valdrían	valieron	valieran	valiesen	
vería	vi	viera	viese	
verías	viste	vieras	vieses	ve
vería	vió	viera	viese	
veríamos	vimos	viéramos	viésemos	
veríais	visteis	vierais	vieseis	ved
verían	vieron	vieran	viesen	

B. *Translate:* 1. We will go out. 2. They have seen. 3. They fell (*pret.*). 4. I conduct. 5. We heard (*pret.*). 6. I go. 7. I am. 8. He would be worth (*cond.*). 9. You (*fam. sing.*) were seeing. 10. We brought (*pret.*). 11. I give. 12. We were going. 13. He was (*imperfect*). 14. You (*fam. sing.*) gave (*pret.*). 15. They will see. 16. I bring. 17. They heard (*pret.*). 18. He would go out (*cond.*). 19. I fall. 20. They conducted (*pret.*).

C. *Translate, using the correct forms of the subjunctive:* **Es lástima que:** 1. He is. 2. We have seen. 3. They hear. 4. You (*fam. sing.*) conducted. 5. We give. 6. They fell. 7. I am going. 8. He went out.

D. *Give the imperatives of* **ir, salir, ser, valer.**

5. RADICAL–CHANGING . . . .

PRESENT INDICATIVE	PRESENT SUBJUNCTIVE	IMPERATIVE	PRESENT PARTICIPLE
CLASS I: **cerrar,** *to close;* **volver,** *to return*			
cierro	cierre	cierra	
cierras	cierres	cerrad	
cierra	cierre		
cerramos	cerremos		
cerráis	cerréis		
cierran	cierren		
vuelvo	vuelva	vuelve	
vuelves	vuelvas	volved	
vuelve	vuelva		
volvemos	volvamos		
volvéis	volváis		
vuelven	vuelvan		
CLASS II: **sentir,** *to feel, regret;* **dormir,** *to sleep*			
siento	sienta	siente	sintiendo
sientes	sientas	sentid	
siente	sienta		
sentimos	sintamos		
sentís	sintáis		
sienten	sientan		
duermo	duerma	duerme	durmiendo
duermes	duermas	dormid	
duerme	duerma		
dormimos	durmamos		
dormís	durmáis		
duermen	duerman		
CLASS III: **pedir,** *to ask for*			
pido	pida	pide	pidiendo
pides	pidas	pedid	
pide	pida		
pedimos	pidamos		
pedís	pidáis		
piden	pidan		

GRAMMAR

A. Radical-changing verbs are usually divided into three classes. Verbs of Class I are identified in the vocabulary of this book like this: **cerrar (ie), volver (ue)**; verbs of Class II: **sentir (ie, i), dormir (ue, u)**; verbs of Class III: **pedir (i)**. *Study the model conjugations.*

PRETERITE INDICATIVE	I. IMPERFECT SUBJUNCTIVE	II. IMPERFECT SUBJUNCTIVE
. . . . CLASS I		
. . . . CLASS II		
sentí	sintiera	sintiese
sentiste	sintieras	sintieses
sintió	sintiera	sintiese
sentimos	sintiéramos	sintiésemos
sentisteis	sintierais	sintieseis
sintieron	sintieran	sintiesen
dormí	durmiera	durmiese
dormiste	durmieras	durmieses
durmió	durmiera	durmiese
dormimos	durmiéramos	durmiésemos
dormisteis	durmierais	durmieseis
durmieron	durmieran	durmiesen
pedí	pidiera	pidiese
pediste	pidieras	pidieses
pidió	pidiera	pidiese
pedimos	pidiéramos	pidiésemos
pedisteis	pidierais	pidieseis
pidieron	pidieran	pidiesen

B. The vowel changes may be summarized as follows:

CLASS I. Verbs ending in –**ar** and –**er** change **e** to **ie** or **o** to **ue** in all persons of the singular and in the third person plural of the present indicative and subjunctive. The same changes occur in the singular imperative.

[17]

Class II. Certain verbs ending in –ir show the same changes as in Class I plus a change of e to i or o to u in the present participle, the first and second persons plural of the present subjunctive, both third persons of the preterite, and all persons of the imperfect subjunctive.

Class III. Certain other verbs ending in –ir change e to i in all the persons and tenses affected in Classes I and II.

C. The following common radical-changing verbs are used in the exercises of this lesson. For meanings, see the Vocabulary.

Class I: Acostarse, contar, despertar, encender, encontrar, entender, jugar, mostrar, mover, negar, oler,* pensar, perder, recordar, rogar, sentarse.

Class II: Advertir, consentir, divertirse, morir, preferir.

Class III: Despedir, elegir, impedir, reír, reñir,† repetir, servir, vestirse.

EXERCISES

A. *Fill in blanks with the proper vowel or diphthong* (e, ie, i, o, ue, u), *and translate. Add written accent if required.* 1. (acostarse) Me ac—sto. 2. (dormir) D—rme. 3. (cerrar) C—rramos. 4. (pedir) P—den. 5. (pensar) P—nsas. 6. (repetir) Rep—támoslo. 7. (reñir) ¡ No r—ña usted ! 8. (sentarse) ¡ S—ntense ustedes ! 9. (divertirse) ¡ Que os div—rtáis ! 10. (morir) Estoy m—riendo. 11. (despedir) Desp—diendo. 12. (advertir) Lo adv—rtieron. 13. (perder) Lo p—rdieron. 14. (reír) R—ó. 15. (consentir) Quería que cons—ntiéramos. 16. (elegir) No quería que ella lo el—giera. 17. (volver) V—lvió. 18. (preferir) Pref—rió. 19. (encender) ¡ Enc—ndala usted ! 20. (impedir) ¡ Imp—dámoslo !

B. *Translate:* 1. I count. 2. They regret. 3. He serves. 4. You (*fam. sing.*) remember. 5. We have a good time. 6. Laughing. 7. **Quiere que** we get dressed (*pres. subj.*). 8. **Quería que** I should consent (*imp. subj.*). 9. We lost (*pret.*). 10. **Quiere que** they understand (*pres. subj.*). 11. He dismissed (*pret.*). 12. Dying. 13. **Quieren que** you (*fam. pl.*) notice (*pres. subj.*). 14. They slept (*pret.*). 15. They deny. 16. **Quieren que** I sit down (*pres. subj.*). 17. Showing. 18. **Quieren que** I play (*pres. subj.*). 19. You (*fam. sing.*) find. 20. They smell.

---

* **Oler** requires an h before **ue: huelo, hueles, huele,** olemos, oléis, **huelen.**
† Verbs whose stems end in **ñ** (or **ll**) drop the i of the diphthongs ie and io.

6. ORTHOGRAPHIC CHANG-
ING VERBS • • • • • • • • • • • •

PRESENT INDICATIVE	PRESENT SUBJUNCTIVE	PRESENT INDICATIVE	PRESENT SUBJUNCTIVE
1. −ger or −gir: coger		2. −guir: distinguir	
cojo	coja	distingo	distinga
coges	cojas	distingues	distingas
coge	coja	distingue	distinga
cogemos	cojamos	distinguimos	distingamos
cogéis	cojáis	distinguís	distingáis
cogen	cojan	distinguen	distingan
3. CONSONANT + −cer or −cir vencer		4. VOWEL + −cer or −cir conocer	
venzo	venza	conozco	conozca
vences	venzas	conoces	conozcas
vence	venza	conoce	conozca
vencemos	venzamos	conocemos	conozcamos
vencéis	venzáis	conocéis	conozcáis
vencen	venzan	conocen	conozcan

PRESENT SUBJUNCTIVE	PRETERITE INDICATIVE	PRESENT SUBJUNCTIVE	PRETERITE INDICATIVE
5. −car: buscar		6. −gar: llegar	
busque	busqué	llegue	llegué
busques	buscaste	llegues	llegaste
busque	buscó	llegue	llegó
busquemos	buscamos	lleguemos	llegamos
busquéis	buscasteis	lleguéis	llegasteis
busquen	buscaron	lleguen	llegaron
7. −guar: averiguar		8. −zar: alcanzar	
averigüe	averigüé	alcance	alcancé
averigües	averiguaste	alcances	alcanzaste
averigüe	averiguó	alcance	alcanzó
averigüemos	averiguamos	alcancemos	alcanzamos
averigüéis	averiguasteis	alcancéis	alcanzasteis
averigüen	averiguaron	alcancen	alcanzaron

GRAMMAR

A. Study the forms of the eight types of orthographic-changing verbs that are given. Note that with the exception of **conocer**, the model verbs are absolutely *regular*, as pronounced. The spelling changes are required in order to maintain the regularity of pronunciation.

1. **coger**, *to seize, catch*
2. **distinguir**, *to distinguish*
3. **vencer**, *to conquer*
4. **conocer**, *to be acquainted with, to know*
5. **buscar**, *to look for*
6. **llegar**, *to arrive*
7. **averiguar**, *to verify*
8. **alcanzar**, *to overtake, to reach*

B. The spelling changes of the model verbs may be summarized as follows:

INFINITIVE	CHANGE	BEFORE	IN
1. –ger or –gir	g to j	o AND a	1st Sing. PRESENT INDICATIVE AND *All* PRESENT SUBJUNCTIVE
2. –guir	gu to g		
3. CONSONANT + { –cer / –cir	c to z		
4. VOWEL + { –cer / –cir	c to zc		

EXAMPLES:

1. **–ger** or **–gir**: **coger, escoger, recoger, dirigir, exigir.**
2. **–guir**: **distinguir, seguir.** (**Seguir** is also radical-changing.)
3. CONSONANT + **–cer** or **–cir**: **vencer, esparcir.**
4. VOWEL + **–cer** or **–cir**: **conocer, ofrecer, conducir, producir.** (**Conducir** and **producir** are irregular in the preterite and the imperfect subjunctive. See conjugation of **conducir** in Chapter IV.)

INFINITIVE	CHANGE	BEFORE	IN
5. –car	c to qu	e	*All* PRESENT SUBJUNCTIVE AND 1st Singular PRETERITE INDICATIVE
6. –gar	g to gu		
7. –guar	gu to gü		
8. –zar	z to c		

EXAMPLES:

5. –car: buscar, sacar, tocar.
6. –gar: llegar, pagar, rogar.   (**Rogar** is also radical-changing, **ue**.)
7. –guar: averiguar.
8. –zar: alcanzar, cruzar, gozar.

EXERCISES

A. *Translate, using the correct forms of the present and preterite indicative:* 1. I arrived. 2. I follow. 3. I played (*the piano*). 4. I catch. 5. I crossed. 6. I direct. 7. I ascertained. 8. I conquer. 9. I know. 10. I conduct.

B. *Translate, using the correct forms of the present subjunctive:* **Quiero que:** 1. He looks for. 2. They pick up. 3. She pays. 4. You (*fam. sing.*) demand. 5. He overtakes. 6. They distinguish. 7. You ascertain. 8. He scatters. 9. They produce. 10. You (*fam. sing.*) offer.

C. *Change each of the following forms to the present subjunctive and to the preterite, and state in each case why a consonant change is or is not required:* 1. Escoge. 2. Distingo. 3. Producen. 4. Tocamos. 5. Averiguo. 6. Pagas. 7. Cruzo. 8. Vence. 9. Conocemos. 10. Recojo.

7. OTHER ORTHOGRAPHIC— .

PRESENT PARTICIPLE	PRESENT INDICATIVE	PRESENT SUBJUNCTIVE

A. VERBS ENDING IN –uir: huir, to flee . . . .

huyendo	huyo	huya
	huyes	huyas
	huye	huya
	huimos	huyamos
	huís	huyáis
	huyen	huyan

B. VERBS ENDING IN –eer: creer, to believe, think . . . .

creyendo	[REGULAR]	[REGULAR]

C. VERBS ENDING IN –iar: enviar, to send . . . .

[REGULAR]	envío	envíe
	envías	envíes
	envía	envíe
	enviamos	enviemos
	enviáis	enviéis
	envían	envíen

D. VERBS ENDING IN –uar: continuar, to continue . . . .

[REGULAR]	continúo	continúe
	continúas	continúes
	continúa	continúe
	continuamos	continuemos
	continuáis	continuéis
	continúan	continúen

GRAMMAR

A. Verbs ending in –uir (except –guir and –quir) substitute y for unstressed i between vowels, and insert y before all endings except those beginning with i.

OTHER EXAMPLES: **concluir, construir, destruir.**

B. Verbs ending in –eer substitute y for unstressed i between vowels. This change occurs in the present participle, both third persons of the preterite, all forms of the imperfect subjunctive. Note that the stressed i of these verbs requires a written accent.

[22]

PRETERITE INDICATIVE	I. IMPERFECT SUBJUNCTIVE	II. IMPERFECT SUBJUNCTIVE
		–uir
huí	huyera	huyese
huiste	huyeras	huyeses
huyó	huyera	huyese
huimos	huyéramos	huyésemos
huisteis	huyerais	huyeseis
huyeron	huyeran	huyesen
		–eer
creí	creyera	creyese
creíste	creyeras	creyeses
creyó	creyera	creyese
creímos	creyéramos	creyésemos
creísteis	creyerais	creyeseis
creyeron	creyeran	creyesen

OTHER EXAMPLES: **leer, poseer.** Although their infinitives do not end in –eer, **oír** and **caer** show the same changes.

C. Certain verbs ending in –iar (but not **cambiar, estudiar, limpiar**) require a written accent on the **i** throughout the singular and in the third person plural of the present indicative and subjunctive.

OTHER EXAMPLES: **confiar, fiar, guiar, variar.**

D. Verbs ending in –uar (except **–guar**) require a written accent on the **u** throughout the singular and in the third person plural of the present indicative and subjunctive.

OTHER EXAMPLES: **actuar, acentuar.**

EXERCISES

A. *Change the following forms to the third person plural of the preterite, and translate:* 1. Leo. 2. Huyo. 3. Confío. 4. Continúo. 5. Construyo. 6. Creo. 7. Guío. 8. Concluyo. 9. Varío. 10. Destruyo.

B. *Translate:* 1. Reading. 2. He heard (*pret.*). 3. They destroyed (*pret.*). 4. We believed (*pret.*). 5. It varies. 6. **Queremos que** they continue (*pres. subj.*). 7. **Quiero que** he flees, they send, we guide (*pres. subj.*). 8. **No queríamos que** they should flee (*imp. subj.*).

[23]

8. PRESENT, FUTURE
& CONDITIONAL . . . .

GRAMMAR

The various tenses of the Spanish verb show uses that differ somewhat from their English equivalents. However, only the truly essential differences are discussed in this and the following lessons.

A. THE PRESENT INDICATIVE. I. The present is regularly used to express affirmation, negation, and interrogation and does not need auxiliaries such as "is," "does," "doesn't."

(*a*) **Estudia.** He studies, he is studying, *or* he does study.
(*b*) ¿ **No estudia?** Isn't he studying?

II. Especially in conversation, the present tense is used to express an immediate future. Its use with this meaning is particularly common when accompanied by an adverb indicating future time, or in questions involving the near future.

(*a*) **Vuelvo en seguida.** I'll be right back.
(*b*) ¿ **Nos vamos?** Shall we leave?

III. The present is used to indicate that an action or state begun at a definite time in the past is still in progress in the present.

(*a*) **Hace días que te busco.** I have been looking for you for days.
(*b*) **Estoy aquí desde ayer.** I have been here since yesterday.

B. THE FUTURE INDICATIVE. I. The future is used to express inference (probability).

(*a*) ¿ **Qué hora será?** I wonder what time it is?
(*b*) ¿ **Quién habla? Será el portero.** Who is talking? It's probably (I suppose it's) the doorman.

II. The future must NOT be used to translate "will," to express *willingness*. Use **querer** to express *willingness*.

¿ Quiere Vd. pasarme la sal? Will you pass me the salt?

[24]

C. The Conditional. I. The conditional is used to express future time in relation to a particular past time.

Dijo que vendría. He said he would come.

II. It is used to express inference in past time.

¿ Quién hablaba? Sería el portero. Who was talking? It was probably the doorman.

EXERCISES

A. *Restate the following sentences in the past, and translate:* 1. Dice que lo hará. 2. ¿ Quién habla? Será tu hermano. 3. Le escribiré. 4. ¿ Qué hora será? 5. Juan afirma que lo tendrá para el lunes.

B. *Translate:* 1. It is time to eat. Shall I call the children? 2. He says he is studying law. I don't believe it. 3. If you cry, I'll leave. 4. We have been working for two weeks. 5. He says he will arrive on time. 6. He said he would arrive on time. 7. I have been here since last week. 8. Who can that man be? 9. Who do you suppose that man was? 10. Will you close the door? 11. We'll leave at once. 12. My son has been attending this school for three years. 13. Who was talking to your sister in the café yesterday? 14. It must have been our cousin.

9. IMPERFECT & PRETERITE . . .

GRAMMAR

The imperfect and preterite express different views of past actions or states. The most important function of the imperfect is to describe; the most important function of the preterite, to narrate.

A. THE IMPERFECT INDICATIVE. I. The imperfect is often combined in a single sentence with the preterite. The imperfect then expresses action or state of unreported duration in progress at the time something else happened.

(*a*) **Llovía cuando desperté esta mañana.** It was raining when I awoke this morning.

(*b*) **Era junio cuando llegamos a Chile.** It was June when we reached Chile.

II. Time of day in the past is always expressed by the imperfect.

Eran las nueve en punto cuando arrancó el tren. It was nine o'clock sharp when the train pulled out.

III. When the imperfect is combined in a single sentence with another imperfect, both express past actions of unspecified duration occurring at the same time.

Mientras yo estudiaba, mi hermana tocaba el piano. While I was studying, my sister played the piano.

IV. The imperfect is used to report habitual or indefinitely repeated past actions. In English this kind of action is often expressed by *used to* or *would*.

De joven cazaba todos los días. As a young man he used to go hunting every day.

V. In indirect discourse, the imperfect is used to represent the present of direct discourse.

(*a*) **Pepe dijo: — Me voy.** Joe said, "I'm leaving."

(*b*) **Pepe dijo que se iba.** Joe said he was leaving.

B. THE PRETERITE INDICATIVE. I. The preterite is used to express a single action or unit of connected actions viewed as a completed or unified whole.

(*a*) **Leyó la carta.** He read the letter.

(*b*) **En el siglo XVI los españoles lucharon repetidas veces contra los franceses.** In the sixteenth century the Spaniards fought many times against the French.

II. The preterite is used to express past state when the duration of the state is expressed or implied.

Estuvo enfermo todo el verano. He was sick all summer.

III. The duration, whether stated or implied, may be short or long (extended duration does not necessarily require the imperfect).

(*a*) **El peligro no duró más que un instante.** The danger lasted only an instant.
(*b*) **La edad neolítica duró miles de años.** The Neolithic Age lasted thousands of years.

IV. The preterite is used to mark the beginning of a state.

Ayer conocí a Pedro. Yesterday I met Peter.
(Other common preterites in this group are: **supe,** *I learned;* **tuve,** *I got* or *received.*)

V. The preterite is used to indicate a state expressed in definite action.

Pude forzar la puerta. I managed to force open the gate.
(Other common preterites in this group are: **quise,** *I tried;* **no quise,** *I refused.*)

EXERCISES

A. *Rewrite, and fill the blanks with the proper forms of the imperfect and preterite of the verbs in parentheses, and translate into English:*
Caminaba Pedro a un pueblo apartado de la Sierra. La noche (acercarse) — obscura y tormentosa. El solitario caminante (andar) — ensimismado y sin hacer el menor caso de la lluvia que ya (caer) — ni de los truenos que (retumbar) — a lo lejos. De pronto (oírse) — un estampido que le (sacar) — de su abstracción. Pedro (detenerse) — preso de un vago temor y luego (darse) — cuenta de que (encontrarse) — en un paraje famoso por los bandidos que lo (infestar) —.

B. *Translate:* 1. It was seven o'clock when he returned home. 2. The mailman said that our friend was sick. 3. When he lived in Madrid, he would go to the café every afternoon. 4. In December the Spanish Prime Minister made three trips to London. 5. I used to study my lessons while my father read the paper. 6. Yesterday I got (**tener**) a letter from my mother. 7. It was very cold when I left the movies. 8. She refused to accompany me to the dance. 9. Last week I met Antonio Gómez. 10. The Roman Empire lasted about four hundred years.

10. INFINITIVE . . . .

GRAMMAR

The infinitive is a verbal noun. Ordinarily it retains the functions of both noun and verb. Some infinitives, however, may lose their verbal force and be used as common nouns: **el deber,** *duty;* **el poder,** *power;* etc.

A. The infinitive may serve as subject, object, or predicate noun. It is sometimes preceded by the masculine article.

(*a*) **El perder a su amigo le entristeció.** Losing his friend made him very sad.
(*b*) **Quiero ir a Méjico.** I want to go to Mexico.
(*c*) **Saber es poder.** To know how is to be able (Knowledge is power).

B. The infinitive (not the present participle) is used regularly after prepositions.

(*a*) **Tienen ganas de acostarse.** They feel like going to bed.
(*b*) **Después de vestirme, salí a la calle.** After getting dressed, I went out into the street.

C. The infinitive is especially common in time phrases introduced by **al.**

Al volver a Cuba, me dediqué a los negocios. On returning to Cuba, I devoted myself to business.

D. Many verbs take a dependent infinitive without preposition. In this construction the infinitive normally has the same subject as the main verb. Common examples: **deber, esperar, poder, querer, saber, soler.**

(*a*) **Espero salir bien en el examen.** I hope to pass the examination.
(*b*) **Ella sabe tocar la guitarra.** She knows how to play the guitar.

E. Certain verbs of causing, permitting, and perceiving take an infinitive without a preceding preposition even when there is a change of subject. The logical subject of the infinitive is usually regarded as direct object of the main verb. Common examples: **dejar, hacer, oír, ver.**

(*a*) **Dejó salir a los muchachos. Los dejó salir.** He let the boys go out. He let them go out.

[28]

(*b*) **Vimos llegar el barco. Lo vimos llegar.** We saw the boat arrive. We saw it arrive.

F. Many common verbs require a preposition when followed by an infinitive. Such verbs and prepositions must be learned as met. Ten examples of great frequency: **acabar de, atreverse a, comenzar a, dejar de, empezar a, ir a, ponerse a, tardar en, tratar de, venir a.**

EXERCISES

A. *Supply the correct preposition, if one is necessary, and translate:*
1. Trataron — describir la escena. 2. No se atrevieron — mirarnos. 3. Me gusta — nadar. 4. Suele — trabajar por la noche. 5. Deben — estudiarlo otra vez. 6. El niño dejó — llorar. 7. Su padre le dejó — salir. 8. Fué — visitarla. 9. Empiezan — comprender el problema. 10. Cuando llegué, acababan — comer.

B. *Translate:* 1. I always drink a glass of milk before going to bed. 2. He could hear the singing of the birds in the branches. 3. Living in Granada is very pleasant. 4. On arriving home, he read the newspaper. 5. I believe I know what you mean. 6. He had (*use* **hacer**) the doctor come at once. 7. She began to prepare the child's dinner. 8. After crossing the bridge, he left the road. 9. We heard Bidú Sayão sing. 10. At present it is difficult to save money. 11. What you ask me is not in my power. 12. His mother let him go to the movies.

11. PARTICIPLES . . . .

GRAMMAR

A. THE PRESENT PARTICIPLE. Regular present participles (sometimes called gerunds) are formed by adding –ando to the stem of –ar verbs, and –iendo to the stem of –er and –ir verbs: **comprando, comiendo, recibiendo.**

In Spanish, the present participle always has verbal force. Hence, it can never be used as a simple noun or adjective, that is, for example, as a translation of *hunting* in such an expression as "hunting is his favorite sport," or *running* in "running water in every room."

I. The present participle is frequently used to modify the subject of a verb. It expresses attendant circumstance or some aspect of the main action. If its subject is expressed, it follows the participle.

(*a*) **Estando Juan en el extranjero, no pudo pasar las Navidades con su familia.** Since John was abroad, he couldn't spend Christmas with his family.

(*b*) **Teniendo salud, puede Vd. hacer cualquier cosa.** If you are healthy you can do anything.

(*c*) **Salió corriendo del edificio.** He ran out of the building.

II. One of the more useful functions of the present participle as a modifier is to express the means by which something is accomplished.

Leyendo día y noche adquirió una cultura asombrosa. By reading day and night he acquired an astonishing culture.

III. With a few verbs (particularly verbs of sense perception), the present participle may be used to modify the object of the verb. Compare with **E,** Chap. 10.

La vi bailando. I saw her dancing.

IV. The present participle is used in the formation of progressive tenses. For this usage, see Chap. 18.

B. THE PAST PARTICIPLE. The chief use of the past participle is to form the compound tenses. (Another important use is to form the passive of action or state, treated in Chap. 18.)

I. The past participle is frequently found in absolute constructions.

(*a*) **Firmada la petición, todos se marcharon.** The petition having been signed, all left.

(*b*) **Hecho esto, cada uno volvió a casa.** This being done, each one returned home.

II. The past participle is often used as an adjective with either active or passive meaning.

(*a*) **El suelo cubierto de flores** ... The ground covered with flowers ...

(*b*) **El hombre acostado en el sofá** ... The man lying on the sofa ...

III. Some past participles commonly used as simple adjectives are:

aficionado,* *fond of*	**cansado,** *tiresome*	**enamorado,** *in love, enamored*
agradecido, *grateful*	**divertido,** *amusing*	**sentado,** *sitting*
atrevido, *bold*	**dormido,** *asleep, sleeping*	**sufrido,** *long-suffering*
callado, *silent*		

EXERCISES

A. *Translate:* 1. The man sitting in the chair. 2. A grateful woman. 3. A sleeping child. 4. An amusing comedy. 5. A house surrounded by trees.

B. *Translate:* 1. He ran into the room. 2. By studying hard you will learn Spanish. 3. He heard her singing in the garden. 4. When I was in Mexico, I met Alfonso Reyes. 5. I am (**ser**) fond of Italian music. 6. Once the problem was solved, we talked of other things. 7. The fans applauded the bullfighter. 8. A man in love often acts like a fool. 9. He ran up the stairs. *Imitate A, I(c), p. 30.* 10. The trip was very tiresome.

* Past participles are also used as nouns (see Chap. 23, B, I). **Aficionado** is very common as a noun meaning *fan* or *devotee*.

[31]

12. REFLEXIVES • • • • • • • • • •

GRAMMAR

A. A reflexive verb is one whose action or state operates on the subject ("He cut himself"). Sense permitting, any transitive verb may be made reflexive by adding the reflexive pronouns: **me, te, se, nos, os, se**:

TRANSITIVE VERB: **Juan levanta la mano.** John raises his hand.
USED REFLEXIVELY: **Juan se levanta.** John rises (gets up).

The reflexive pronoun may be either direct or indirect object:

DIRECT OBJECT: **Me bañé.** I bathed myself (took a bath).
INDIRECT OBJECT: **Me compré un libro.** I bought myself a book.

B. Memorize the following list of transitive verbs commonly used reflexively. Note that many of them acquire intransitive force.

acercarse (a), *to approach*
acordarse (de), *to remember*
casarse (con), *to marry*
detenerse, *to stop*
dirigirse (a), *to address, head for*
encontrarse, *to find oneself, be*
fijarse en, *to notice*
hacerse, * *to become*
levantarse, *to get up, rise*
llamarse, *to be called* (**se llama Juan,** *his name is John*)
meterse (en), *to enter, meddle*
ponerse,† *to become*
presentarse, *to appear, show up*
sentarse, *to sit down*
tratarse (de), *to be a question of*
volverse, *to turn around* (**volverse loco,** *to go crazy*)

C. A number of intransitive verbs may be used reflexively or non-reflexively. In some cases it is easy to express the difference in meaning:

ir, *to go*
marchar, *to march, walk*
parecer, *to seem, appear*
reír, *to laugh*

irse, *to go away*
marcharse, *to leave*
parecerse (a), *to resemble*
reírse (de), *to laugh at*

---

* **Hacerse** is used with a noun or adjective to express voluntary becoming: **Se hizo rico.** *He became rich.* † **Ponerse** is used with an adjective or past participle to express involuntary change of state or condition: **Se puso enfermo.** *He became sick.*

In some other cases the difference is not easily translated. The following suggested translations are at best only partially successful:

callar, *to be silent*	**callarse,** *to be silent, not answer*
morir, *to die*	**morirse,** *to die* (a natural death)
quedar, *to remain, be left behind*	**quedarse,** *to remain, stay behind* (*voluntarily*)

D. A few verbs are always used reflexively. The most common are: **atreverse (a),** *to dare* and **quejarse (de),** *to complain.*

E. The reflexive verb may be used to express reciprocal action.

Nos vemos todos los días. We see each other every day.

F. The reflexive construction is often used to translate the passive voice when the subject is a thing and no agent is expressed.

(*a*) **Aquí se habla español.** Spanish is spoken here.
(*b*) **En todas partes se venden periódicos.** Newspapers are sold everywhere.
(*c*) **A lo lejos se ve la torre.** The tower can be (is) seen in the distance.

G. The impersonal reflexive is used to translate the English indefinite subjects *one, they, you, people.*

(*a*) **Se dice que habrá guerra.** They say there will be war.
(*b*) **¿ Por dónde se va a la estación?** How do you get to the station?

H. The reflexive construction (3rd person singular only) may take a personal object.

Se invitó al presidente. The president was invited.

I. The same idea is often expressed by the indefinite 3rd person plural.

Invitaron al presidente. The president was invited.

EXERCISES

A. *Translate the English phrases by using the appropriate verbs from paragraphs* **B, C, D:** 1. Juan (*will show up*) pronto. 2. Los estudiantes (*are*) sin dinero. 3. Al oír el grito, la muchacha (*turned*) pálida. 4. Muchos poetas (*have gone*) locos. 5. Yo (*don't remember*) su dirección. 6. Las muchachas (*get married*) jóvenes en España. 7. Felipe (*stopped*) a encender un cigarrillo. 8. El policía (*headed for*) la casa del criminal. 9. Para las once todos (*had left*). 10. María

(*resembles*) a su madre. 11. Mi hermano quiere (*remain*) en casa.
12. Los políticos (*don't dare meddle*) en ese asunto.

B. *Translate:* 1. My girl friend and I used to write to each other every day. 2. She would complain when I failed to write her. 3. How do you get to the post office ? 4. From the hotel the Sierra Nevada can be seen (*don't translate "can"*). 5. Pepe Morales used to work at the airport. 6. Yesterday he was fired (*translate two ways*). 8. In Paris books are sold on the banks of the river Seine. 9. After seating the children, he sat down himself. 10. They say that Russian is very difficult.

13. SUBJUNCTIVE. . . . .

MAIN CLAUSES . . . .

A. The subjunctive supplies all command forms* except the affirmative familiar imperatives (**compra, comprad; bebe, bebed; escribe, escribid**). There are three kinds of commands, called: (1) direct; (2) indirect, and (3) hortative:

(1) DIRECT COMMANDS

FORMAL (affir. & neg.)

(*a*) (**No**) **compre, beba, escriba usted.**
(*b*) (**No**) **compren, beban, escriban ustedes.**

FAMILIAR (neg.)

(*c*) **No compres, bebas, escribas.**
(*d*) **No compréis, bebáis, escribáis.**

(2) INDIRECT COMMANDS.

(*a*) **Que entre.** Let him come in.
(*b*) **Que se vayan.** Let them go away.

NOTE: **Que entre** means "Let him come in" in the sense of "have him come in," and is thus different from **déjele entrar**, which means "let" in the sense of "allow, permit."

(3) HORTATIVE COMMANDS.

Cantemos. Let us sing.

NOTE: In conversation, this idea is more often expressed by **vamos a** infinitive: **Vamos a cantar.** Let us sing.

B. The subjunctive is often used to express a wish:

(*a*) **Cúmplase la voluntad del cielo.** Heaven's will be done.
(*b*) ¡ **Viva la República !** Long live the Republic!
(*c*) ¡ **Que se divierta Vd. !** (I hope you) have a good time!
(*d*) ¡ **Quién tuviera la suerte de Juan !** I wish I had John's luck! (**Quién** is used in this way only with the first person singular.)
(*e*) ¡ **Ojalá pudiéramos ir a la playa !** I wish we could go to the beach!

* Command forms combined with object pronouns are treated in Chap. 25.

[35]

C. The subjunctive is used in sentences introduced by a word meaning "perhaps" (**acaso, quizás, tal vez**) when there is strong doubt in the mind of the speaker.

Acaso sea verdad. Perhaps it is true.

EXERCISES

A. *Change the following familiar imperatives to formal commands:*
1. Mira el cielo. 2. Llamad a los niños. 3. Permitidme salir. 4. Responde pronto.

B. *Give the negative forms of the following commands and imperatives:*
1. Compra el billete. 2. Corran ustedes. 3. Subid la escalera. 4. Coma usted la manzana. 5. Bebe la leche.

C. *Translate:* 1. I wish he were here! 2. Long live the President! 3. Perhaps your friend is right. 4. I hope you (*formal*) all have a good time! 5. I wish I could spend a year in Spain! 6. Let's eat. 7. Let him (have him) sign the letter. 8. Let (allow) him go with us. 9. Children, read the lesson! 10. Let's go to bed.

14. SUBJUNCTIVE . . . .
NOUN CLAUSES . . . .

GRAMMAR

The subjunctive is used primarily in dependent clauses. It expresses the speaker's attitude toward what is said in the dependent clause. The attitude is usually one of volition, emotion, or uncertainty.

A. The subjunctive is used in noun clauses after certain kinds of verbs and expressions, provided the subjects of the dependent verb and the main verb are different. If they are the same, the infinitive is used:

Quiero ir. (**Yo** is the subject both of **quiero** and of the infinitive **ir**.) I want to go.

Quiero que ellos vayan. (**Yo** is the subject of **quiero**; **ellos** is the subject of **vayan**.) I want them to go.

I. The subjunctive is used most frequently after verbs and expressions conveying notions of volition, causation, command, necessity, and preference. Learn the following common verbs and expressions:

aconsejar, to advise	**importar,** to matter, be important
convenir, to be proper, be advisable	**mandar,** to order, command
decir,* to tell	**ordenar,** to order, command
dejar, to allow, let	**pedir,** to ask, request
desear, to desire	**permitir,** to permit
gustar, to please	**querer,** to want, wish
hacer, to make, have	**rogar,** to request
impedir, to prevent	**ser preciso (necesario),** to be necessary

(*a*) **Conviene que Vd. le escriba en seguida.** It is advisable that you write him at once.

(*b*) **Es preciso que Vd. me diga la verdad.** It is necessary that you tell me the truth.

(*c*) **No permiten que se fume aquí.** They don't permit smoking here.

(*d*) **Me aconsejó que estudiara más.** He advised me to study more.

---

* **Decir** takes the subjunctive only when it expresses a command: *He told me to do it.* Don't be misled by sentences like this: *He said that his brother ought to do it.* In this sentence there is affirmation, not command.

[37]

NOTE: When the infinitive is used in English (thus failing to show what tense is needed in the Spanish dependent clause), remember to use, in the dependent clause, the present subjunctive after a present or future, and the imperfect subjunctive after a preterite or imperfect.

II. The subjunctive is used after verbs and expressions of emotion such as fear, hope, and pleasure. Learn the following:

alegrarse de, *to be glad*   sentir, *to be sorry*   temer, *to fear, be afraid*
esperar, *to hope*   ser lástima, *to be too bad*

(*a*) **Me alegro de que esté Vd. mejor.** I am glad you are better.
(*b*) **Es lástima que no podamos asistir a la corrida.** It's too bad we can't attend the bullfight.

III. The subjunctive is used after verbs and expressions of denial, disbelief, doubt, uncertainty, possibility, impossibility. EXAMPLES

dudar, *to doubt*   parecer mentira, *to be hard to believe*
negar, *to deny*   ser posible (imposible), *to be possible (impossible)*
no creer, *not to believe*

(*a*) **Dudo que él haya hecho lo que dices.** I doubt that he has done what you say.
(*b*) **Parece mentira que los hombres sean tan crueles.** It's hard to believe that men are so cruel.
(*c*) **Es posible que suban aun más los precios.** It's possible that prices may go up even more.

EXERCISES

A. *Supply all appropriate subjunctive forms of the dependent verb, and translate. In some cases good sense will allow only one or two possibilities in the dependent clause; in others, as many as three:* Siento que Vd. esté, haya estado, estuviera enfermo. **I am sorry that you are, have been, were sick.** 1. Niego que nadie lo (hacer). 2. Negué que nadie lo (hacer). 3. Le diré que (venir). 4. Él quería que su padre (retirarse). 5. Sería lástima que Vds. (irse) tan temprano.

B. *Translate:* 1. He asked me to give him ten dollars. 2. I was afraid that someone would find my wallet. 3. It is advisable that you buy a car now. 4. I want to show you my garden. 5. I want you to see my flowers. 6. We don't believe that he will do it. 7. He told me to bring the key. 8. It's hard to believe that you can fly to Europe in one day. 9. He was glad that his friends had left. 10. It is impossible for Spaniards to forget their past.

15. SUBJUNCTIVE . . . .
ADJECTIVE CLAUSES . . . . . .

A. The subjunctive is used in adjective clauses that modify an indefinite, hypothetical, or negative antecedent.

(*a*) **Haré lo que Vd. me diga.** I shall do whatever you tell me to.

(*b*) **Busco una gramática que sea fácil.** I am looking for a grammar which is easy.
COMPARE: **Busco la gramática que te presté.** I am looking for the grammar which I loaned you.

(*c*) **¿ Hay quien quiera otra taza de café ?** Is there anybody who wants another cup of coffee ?

(*d*) **No hay nadie que le iguale.** There is no one to equal him.

B. The subjunctive is used in relative clauses of concession introduced by **por** + ADJECTIVE, or ADVERB + **que,** or by **cualquiera que,** and sometimes after a superlative.

(*a*) **Por fuerte que sea Vd., no podrá hacerlo.** No matter how strong you may be, you won't be able to do it.

(*b*) **Por mucho que estudie, nunca lo sabrá Vd. todo.** No matter how much you study, you'll never know everything.

(*c*) **Cualquiera que sea el resultado, hay que emprender la tarea.** Whatever the result may be, it is necessary to undertake the task.

(*d*) **Miguel Ángel es el genio más asombroso que haya producido el mundo.** Michelangelo is the most amazing genius the world has produced.

EXERCISES

A. *Supply the proper form of the indicative or the subjunctive, and translate:* 1. Pregúnteselo al primer hombre que (pasar). 2. Encontré un cuadro que me (gustar). 3. Quisiera encontrar un cuadro que no (ser) muy caro. 4. ¿ No hay nadie que (querer) ayudarme ? 5. Los que (interesarse), pueden dirigirse al alcalde. 6. Por duro que te (parecer) el trabajo, tienes que acabarlo.

B. *Translate:* 1. Is Mr. Rivera the most learned professor you know ? 2. He is looking for a secretary who speaks Spanish. 3. No matter how important he is, I can't wait for him. 4. Is there anyone who (**quien**) wants to go to the movies with me ? 5. We will do whatever you advise us. 6. Do you have a pen which you can lend me ? 7. I have the pen which you lent me.

16. SUBJUNCTIVE · · · · · · ·
ADVERBIAL CLAUSES · · · · · ·

GRAMMAR

A. The subjunctive is always used in adverbial clauses expressing purpose, unaccomplished result, proviso, exception, supposition, and imaginative comparison. The possible conjunctions are many. Memorize the following common ones:

para que, *in order that, so that*   con tal (de) que, *provided*
a fin de que, *in order that, so that*   a menos que, *unless*
de modo que, *so that*   supuesto que, *supposing that*
de manera que, *so that*   como si, *as if*
sin que, *without*

(*a*) **Para que haya gobiernos buenos, hacen falta ciudadanos buenos.** Good citizens are needed in order that there be good governments.
(*b*) **Iremos a la playa con tal que haga buen tiempo.** We will go to the beach provided the weather is good.
(*c*) **El ladrón salió sin que le viéramos.** The thief left without our seeing him.
NOTE: If there is no change of subject, use **sin** followed by the infinitive: **El ladrón salió sin hacer ruido.** The thief left without making any noise.
(*d*) **Iremos todos a menos que llueva.** We'll all go unless it rains.
(*e*) **Corría el muchacho como si le persiguiera el diablo.** The boy ran as if the devil were pursuing him.

B. The subjunctive is used in temporal clauses (clauses of time) which are future in relation to the time of the main verb. (*E.g.:* I hit him before he knew it.) Learn the following common conjunctions:

antes (de) que (*always takes subj.*) *before*   en cuanto, *as soon as*
después (de) que, *after*   hasta que, *until*
cuando, *when*   mientras (que), *while*

(*a*) **Salgamos antes que nos vean.** Let's leave before they see us.
(*b*) **Mientras pueda, seguiré luchando.** While I can, I will keep on fighting.
(*c*) **Cuando llegue su prima, jugaremos a los naipes.** When your cousin arrives, we'll play cards.
COMPARE: **Cuando llegó, jugamos a los naipes.** When she arrived, we played cards.

C. The subjunctive is used in clauses of concession unless the statement is given as objective fact. The only conjunction of concession of high frequency is **aunque,** *although, even though.*

Me marcho mañana aunque llueva a cántaros. I'm leaving tomorrow even though it pours.
   COMPARE: **Aunque está lloviendo ahora, voy a salir.** Although it is raining now, I'm going out.
NOTE: Even though the concessive clause contains an acknowledged fact, the subjunctive is often used under the stress of emotion: **Aunque sea Vd. el alcalde, no puede hablarme así.** *Even though you're the mayor, you can't talk to me that way.*

EXERCISES

A. *If necessary, change the infinitive to the proper form of the indicative or subjunctive; then translate the entire sentence:* 1. Aunque (tener) un millón de dólares, yo no le daría nada. 2. Voy a Wáshington para (ver) al Presidente. 3. A menos que Vd. le (invitar), él no asistirá a la fiesta. 4. Me miraba como si me (conocer). 5. En cuanto (acabar) la función, iremos a casa. 6. Aunque yo ya (tener) un buen puesto aquí, me gustaría vivir en Hawai. 7. Hable Vd. de modo que le (oír) los de la última fila. 8. Cuando Pepe (graduarse), se dedicó a los negocios. 9. Antes que (terminarse) la carretera, empezó a crecer el pueblo. 10. Pienso quedarme en Sevilla hasta que (empezar) la feria.

B. *Translate:* 1. Even though you are my friend, I can't help you in this affair. 2. We spoke to the boss so that he would remember us the next day. 3. Write me as soon as you get to Madrid. 4. We played tennis until he came for us. 5. He opened the door without making a sound. 6. Provided you wake up on time, we can go fishing. 7. He called her as though she were his servant. 8. Even though you were rich, I couldn't accept that money.

17. SUBJUNCTIVE . . . .
CONDITIONAL SENTENCES . .

GRAMMAR

Many combinations of tense and mood are found in conditional sentences. The following rules provide only for the most common types.

A. If the result clause is expressed in the conditional or conditional perfect, the condition (if clause) is expressed in the imperfect or pluperfect subjunctive. The –ra form of the imperfect subjunctive is often used as a substitute for the conditional.

(a) **Si tuviera (tuviese) dinero, compraría (comprara) una casa.** If I had money, I would buy a house.

(b) **Si hubiera (hubiese) tenido dinero, habría (hubiera) comprado una casa.** If I had had money, I would have bought a house.

B. In all other cases use the indicative tenses which the sense requires. (Never use the future or conditional after "if" to state a condition.)

(a) **Si tenemos tiempo esta tarde, vamos a jugar un partido de tenis.** If we have time this afternoon, let's play a game of tennis.

(b) **Le importaba poco si lo hacía mal.** He cared little if (when) he did it badly.

(c) **Si no lo hizo Jorge, no sé quién pudo ser.** If George didn't do it, I don't know who could have.

C. Either half of a conditional sentence is often used alone, particularly in conversation.

(a) **¡ Si él supiera lo que pensamos hacer !** If he only knew what we intend to do!

(b) **¡ Si me lo enseñó él mismo !** Why, he showed it to me himself!

(c) **Hubiera sido mejor abandonar el proyecto.** It would have been better to abandon the project.

EXERCISES

A. *Translate:* 1. If you come to my house, I'll show you the picture. 2. I wouldn't keep so much money on my person. 3. If he had been present, he would have protested. 4. Why, everybody knows that!

5. If that child were mine, I would send him to school. 6. If he had time, he always read the paper before breakfast. 7. We would sit down if there were enough chairs. 8. If he had powerful friends, he never took advantage of their influence. 9. If only (*omit "only"*) you knew how to cook! 10. If anyone had been at home, he would have received you.

B. *Give the proper form of the infinitive in parentheses and translate into English:* 1. Si el profesor no (hablar) tan rápidamente, le entenderíamos. 2. Si Juan no estuviera enfermo, (venir) a verme. 3. Si tengo bastante dinero, (ir) esta noche al café a bailar. 4. Si Luis lo (hacer), no me lo dijo. 5. Si yo lo (recordar), te habría llamado.

18. SER & ESTAR ● ● ● ● ● ● ● ●

GRAMMAR

A. Ser. I. The basic function of **ser** is to establish identity between the subject and the subjective complement (predicate noun or adjective). It is like the mathematical sign of equality ($a = b$).

(*a*) **El señor Pérez es médico.** Mr. Pérez is a doctor.
(*b*) **Saber es poder.** To know how is to be able.
(*c*) **Aquí es donde vivo.** Here is where I live.

II. **Ser** is used to express origin, possession, or material.

(*a*) **Soy de California.** I am from California.
(*b*) **Esta casa es de mi abuelo.** This house belongs to my grandfather.
(*c*) **Mi reloj es de oro.** My watch is gold.

III. When **ser** is used with an adjective, the adjective indicates the class to which the subject belongs or a fundamental characteristic of the subject.

(*a*) **Pedro es mejicano.** Peter is a Mexican.
(*b*) **El hierro es duro.** Iron is hard.
(*c*) **María es pálida.** Mary is pale (*her normal complexion*).

NOTE: **Joven, viejo, rico, pobre,** and **feliz** are ordinarily used with **ser**.

IV. **Ser** is used with the past participle to form the passive voice. The participle agrees in gender and number with the subject. The agent is usually expressed by **por**.

América fué descubierta por Colón. America was discovered by Columbus.

B. Estar. I. The basic function of **estar** is to indicate place or location.

(*a*) **Mi hermano está aquí (en casa, en París).** My brother is here (at home, in Paris).
(*b*) **Granada está en Andalucía.** Granada is in Andalusia.

II. When **estar** is used with an adjective, the adjective expresses a quality or state which is accidental or subject to change under changed conditions.

[44]

(*a*) **María está pálida.** Mary is pale (NOW, *but not typically*).
(*b*) **El suelo está sucio.** The floor is dirty.

III. With adjectives **estar** may stress the personal reaction of the speaker and convey such notions as *feel, look, taste*.

(*a*) ¡ **Qué bonita estás !** How pretty you look !
(*b*) **No estoy bien.** I don't feel well.
(*c*) **Esta sopa está muy buena.** This soup tastes very good.

IV. **Estar** is used with a past participle to express the state or condition in which the subject is found as a result of the action expressed by the participle. The participle agrees with the subject.

(*a*) **Cuando entré en la sala, las ventanas estaban cerradas.** When I entered the living room, the windows were closed. (Someone HAD CLOSED them prior to my entry.)
(*b*) **El palacio está rodeado de árboles.** The palace is surrounded by trees.

V. **Estar** is used with the present participle to form the progressive tenses. It expresses action actually in progress. It is NOT used in such sentences as, "He is going to New York tomorrow." The participle does not agree with the subject.

(*a*) **No le interrumpas. Está escribiendo una carta.** Don't interrupt him. He is writing a letter.
(*b*) **Estuvo jugando toda la noche.** He spent the whole night gambling.

EXERCISES

A. *Supply the correct form of* **ser** *or* **estar :** 1. En aquella región la lluvia — frecuente. 2. — una hermosa mañana de verano. 3. En aquel momento yo debía de — pálido como un muerto. 4. Su casa — de ladrillos. 5. Si no llovía, al día siguiente todo — seco. 6. El hombre necesita poco para — feliz. 7. ¡ Qué hermosa — su novia esta noche ! 8. Su jardín — florecido. 9. La pólvora — inventada por los chinos. 10. Ayer — enferma mi madre.

B. *Translate :* 1. Mr. Castro is a famous doctor. 2. He is from Madrid. 3. He is in New York now. 4. This fresh bread tastes very good. 5. *Don Quixote* was written by Cervantes. 6. When I arrived, everybody was shouting. 7. That new car belongs to his father. 8. The Grand Canyon is in Arizona. 9. The patio is covered with (**de**) leaves. 10. His wife is very young. 11. González is the captain of the team. 12. The best bullfighters are Spaniards and Mexicans.

[45]

19. DEFINITE ARTICLE . . . . .

GRAMMAR

A. Forms of the Definite Article. I. The forms of the definite article are:

MASC.	el	los
FEM.	la	las

II. **El** is used regularly before feminine singular nouns beginning with stressed –a (ha–): **el agua.**

III. The masculine singular form contracts with the prepositions **a** and **de: al, del.**

B. Uses of the Definite Article. I. The definite article is used with abstract nouns and nouns indicating a whole class:

(*a*) **La ciencia domina la vida moderna.** Science dominates modern life.
(*b*) **Los perros son animales fieles.** Dogs are faithful animals.

II. The definite article is used with names of languages (see exceptions under paragraph **C**) and peoples:

(*a*) **El español es una lengua sonora.** Spanish is a sonorous language.
(*b*) **Los italianos son músicos.** Italians are musical.

III. The definite article is used with modified names of persons and places and, except in direct address, with most titles (see exceptions under **C**):

(*a*) **El pobre Juan.** Poor John.
(*b*) **La España medieval.** Medieval Spain.
(*c*) **El señor Alonso.** Mr. Alonso.

IV. Ordinarily the definite article appears with days of the week and other expressions of time:

(*a*) **Saldremos el miércoles.** We'll leave on Wednesday.
(*b*) **Llegué el tres de junio.** I arrived on the third of June.
(*c*) **Eran las cinco.** It was five o'clock.
(*d*) **La semana pasada.** Last week.

V. With parts of the body and articles habitually associated with one's person, the definite article is used (NOT the possessive adjective as in English).

(*a*) **Ella tiene el pelo negro.** Her hair is black.
(*b*) **El niño se quitó los zapatos.** The child took off his shoes.

C. OMISSION OF THE DEFINITE ARTICLE. I. The definite article is omitted before the titles **don, doña, fray, San, sor**:

Don Luis está aquí. Don Louis is here.

II. The definite article is omitted before other titles used in direct address:

Señora Gálvez, ¿ cómo está Vd. ? Mrs. Gálvez, how are you ?

III. The definite article is omitted before most unmodified proper nouns:

Italia es la patria de las artes. Italy is the homeland of the arts.
COMMON EXCEPTIONS: **La Argentina, El Brasil, El Canadá, Los Estados Unidos, La Habana, El Perú.**

IV. After any form of **ser,** the definite article is omitted before the days of the week:

Hoy es lunes. Today is Monday.

V. The definite article is omitted before the name of a language which is the object of the prepositions **de,** or **en,** or of the verbs **hablar, escribir, estudiar,** or **aprender**:

(*a*) **Una carta escrita en español.** A letter written in Spanish.
(*b*) **Hablo ruso.** I speak Russian.

EXERCISES

A. *In the following phrases change everything possible to the singular:*
1. El hijo de los condes. 2. Las aguas de los lagos. 3. ¿ Has enviado las flores a las señoras ? 4. ¿ Y los cigarros a los hombres ? 5. La belleza de las mujeres.

B. *Supply the definite article where required:* 1. A ella le encantan — flores. 2. No suelen separarse — religión y — moral. 3. Hoy nadie ha visto a — doña Pilar. 4. Mañana será — martes. 5. Estu-

diamos — francés.   6. Estuvieron en Cuba — verano pasado.   7. —
leones no son — animales domésticos.

C. *Translate:* 1. Modern Mexico is a progressive country.   2. Last
year there were more tourists than usual.   3. He left with his hat in
his hand.   4. Poor Mary cannot attend the dance.   5. Mrs. González,
do you want another cup of coffee ?   6. They say that Russian is very
difficult.   7. His guest appeared on Thursday.   8. Brazil is a huge
country.

20. INDEFINITE ARTICLE . . . .

GRAMMAR

A. FORMS OF THE INDEFINITE ARTICLE. I. The forms of the indefinite article are:

MASC.	un	unos
FEM.	una	unas

II. **Un** is usually found before a feminine singular noun beginning with stressed **a–** (**ha–**): **un alma.**

B. USES OF THE INDEFINITE ARTICLE. I. The singular form is regularly used to indicate one particular person or thing not yet identified:

Aquel hombre es un amigo mío. That man is a friend of mine.

II. The plural of the indefinite article is used before many nouns as an indefinite adjective meaning "some," before nouns denoting things which occur by two's to indicate "a pair of," and before numerals to mean "about."

(*a*) **Tengo unos libros viejos.** I have some old books.
(*b*) **Unos zapatos nuevos.** A pair of new shoes.
(*c*) **Unos treinta alumnos.** About thirty students.

C. OMISSION OF THE INDEFINITE ARTICLE. I. The indefinite article is usually omitted before an unmodified predicate noun denoting a whole class (occupational, national, political, religious):

(*a*) **Su hermano es ingeniero.** His brother is an engineer.
(*b*) **Nuestro vecino es socialista.** Our neighbor is a socialist.
(*c*) **Concha es peruana.** Concha is a Peruvian.

II. The indefinite article is omitted in negative expressions before nouns used in an indefinite sense. (Spanish has no words equivalent to unstressed English *any* or *no*.):

(*a*) **No tengo dinero.** I have no money (I haven't any money).
(*b*) **Llegó sin sombrero.** He arrived without any hat.
(*c*) **¿ Hay hombre más generoso que Pablo ?** Is there any man more generous than Paul ?

[49]

III. The indefinite article is omitted before nouns modified by the indefinite adjectives **cierto, otro, tal,** and before the numerals **ciento (cien)** and **mil:**

(*a*) **Otra mujer.** Another woman.
(*b*) **Tal hombre.** Such a man.
(*c*) **Cien niños.** A hundred children.

IV. The indefinite article is omitted before nouns used in adjectival phrases:

(*a*) **Una muchacha de ojos azules.** A blue-eyed girl.
(*b*) **Un pañuelo de seda.** A silk handkerchief.

EXERCISES

A. *Supply the indefinite article where needed, and translate:* 1. Pío Baroja es — novelista célebre. 2. No vimos — pájaros en todo el viaje. 3. Su vanidad de — hombre superior es insufrible. 4. Ya te lo he dicho — mil veces. 5. María tiene — ojos hermosos. 6. No hay — asunto más pesado que ése. 7. Su mejor amigo es — suizo.

B. *Translate:* 1. I gave her a gold watch. 2. Such a man does not deserve to be a senator. 3. He owns about twenty horses. 4. Did you say that he is a lawyer? 5. The airplane is a powerful weapon. 6. He sat down without saying a word. 7. His sister-in-law is a Catholic. 8. He has a pair of hands like hams. 9. Don Pablo is a Cuban. 10. He likes black-haired girls.

21. NUMBERS . . . .

GRAMMAR

A. CARDINAL NUMBERS.

0. cero	16. dieciséis (diez y seis)	101. ciento uno
1. un(o), una	17. diecisiete (diez y siete)	110. ciento diez
2. dos	18. dieciocho (diez y ocho)	200. doscientos, –as
3. tres	19. diecinueve (diez y nueve)	300. trescientos, –as
4. cuatro	20. veinte	400. cuatrocientos, –as
5. cinco	21. veintiuno (veinte y uno)	500. quinientos, –as
6. seis	22. veintidós (veinte y dos)	600. seiscientos, –as
7. siete	30. treinta	700. setecientos, –as
8. ocho	31. treinta y uno	800. ochocientos, –as
9. nueve	40. cuarenta	900. novecientos, –as
10. diez	50. cincuenta	1000. mil
11. once	60. sesenta	1010. mil diez
12. doce	70. setenta	2000. dos mil
13. trece	80. ochenta	1,000,000. un millón (de)
14. catorce	90. noventa	3,000,000. tres millones (de)
15. quince	100. cien(to)	

NOTE: **y** (the conjunction *and*) is used ONLY to join tens and digits. Through the *twenties*, the compound numbers are usually written as one word, and the conjunction **y** has the spelling **i: dieciséis, veinticinco,** etc. Above the *thirties*, compound numbers are usually written as separate words: **treinta y seis, setenta y cuatro,** etc. You can, however, with perfect correctness write all these compound numbers as separate words.

I. Among the cardinal numerals the only ones inflected for the feminine are **uno** and the hundreds (200–900):

(*a*) **treinta y una vacas,** thirty-one cows
(*b*) **novecientas diez casas,** nine hundred and ten houses

II. The **o** of **uno** is dropped before masculine nouns. **Ciento** becomes **cien** before any noun or numeral which it multiplies:

(*a*) **un automóvil,** one automobile
(*b*) **cincuenta y un años,** fifty-one years
(*c*) **cien caballos,** one hundred horses
(*d*) **cien mil soldados,** 100,000 soldiers

III. **Un** is omitted before **cien(to)** (*Cf.* II, *c*) and **mil** but not before **millón**. **Millón** is a collective and ordinarily is followed by **de**:

(*a*) **mil estrellas,** a thousand stars
(*b*) **un millón de hombres,** a million men

IV. In expressing dates the cardinals are used except for the first day of the month:

(*a*) ¿ **Qué fecha es hoy?** What is the date today?
(*b*) **Es el primero de mayo.** It is the first of May.
(*c*) **Es el tres de julio.** It is the third of July.

B. Ordinal Numbers.

1st	primer(o)	6th	sexto
2nd	segundo	7th	séptimo
3rd	tercer(o)	8th	octavo
4th	cuarto	9th	noveno
5th	quinto	10th	décimo

I. **Primero** and **tercero** drop **o** before a masculine singular noun: **el primer día.**

II. The ordinals are inflected for gender and number. They precede the noun they modify when used as limiting adjectives; they usually follow when they identify an individual member of a series. Above tenth the cardinals are commonly used instead of the ordinals:

(*a*) **Mis primeras impresiones.** My first impressions.
(*b*) **Carlos Quinto, Alfonso Trece.** Charles V, Alphonso XIII.
(*c*) **El capítulo décimo.** The tenth chapter.

EXERCISES

A. *Read in Spanish:* 1. (*One*) cama. 2. (*Twenty-one*) días. 3. (*One hundred and six*) coches. 4. (*Two million*) dólares. 5. (*One thousand*) aviones. 6. (*One hundred*) muchachas. 7. (*Five hundred*) casas. 8. Carlos (I). 9. Alfonso (XII). 10. El capítulo (IX). 11. (*Three hundred and two*) plumas. 12. (*The third*) mes.

B. *Translate:* 1. What was the date when you arrived? 2. It was the first of April. 3. It is now the nineteenth of June. 4. Last year seven hundred books were lost in the university library. 5. The hospital has seventy-one beds.

22. NOUNS: FORMS . . . .

GRAMMAR

A. GENDER OF NOUNS. All Spanish nouns are either masculine or feminine. The gender of those not covered by the following rules must be learned individually.

I. Nouns ending in **o** are regularly masculine; those ending in **a** are regularly feminine:

el caballo, the horse
el libro, the book

la vaca, the cow
la mesa, the table

COMMON EXCEPTIONS:

el clima, the climate
el día, the day
el idioma, the language
el mapa, the map

el poema, the poem
el poeta, the poet
el sistema, the system
la mano, the hand

II. Regardless of ending, nouns denoting male beings are masculine; those denoting female beings are feminine:

el policía, the policeman
el conductor, the conductor
el padre, the father

la actriz, the actress
la mujer, the woman
la madre, the mother

III. Nouns ending in **–ad, –ud, –ie, –ción (–sión)**, and **–umbre** are feminine:

la ciudad, the city
la bondad, the kindness
la virtud, the virtue

la serie, the series
la lección, the lesson
la muchedumbre, the crowd

B. NUMBER OF NOUNS. I. Nouns ending in a vowel or diphthong add **s** to form the plural:

el perro, the dog   los perros
el papá, the papa   los papás
el café, the cafe   los cafés

la casa, the house   las casas
la especie, the species   las especies
la serie, the series   las series

NOTE: A very few uncommon nouns ending in a stressed vowel add –es: rubí, rubíes, ruby, rubies.

II. Nouns ending in a consonant (including **y**) add **–es** to form the plural:

el papel, the paper   los papeles   el rey, the king   los reyes

III. Nouns with a final unstressed syllable in –es or –is remain unchanged in the plural:

el viernes, the Friday   **los viernes**   **la tesis,** the thesis   **las tesis**

C. ORTHOGRAPHIC CHANGES IN NOUNS.   I. Nouns ending in –z change z to c in the plural: **luz, luces,** light, lights.

II. Nouns with final stressed syllable in –n or –s lose their written accent in the plural:

nación, nation   **naciones**   **revés,** reverse   **reveses**

III. Nouns with final unstressed syllable in –n require a written accent in the plural:

joven, youth   **jóvenes**   **origen,** origin   **orígenes**

EXERCISES

A. *Supply the proper definite article, and indicate which nouns follow the rules for gender, and which must be learned individually:* 1. — ocasión. 2. — frase. 3. — comerciante. 4. — idioma. 5. — dificultad. 6. — serie. 7. — día. 8. — actriz. 9. — juventud. 10. — muchedumbre. 11. — mapa. 12. — paquete.

B. *Give the plural of the following nouns:* 1. El pie. 2. La ley. 3. El lunes. 4. La mujer. 5. El café. 6. La vez. 7. El alemán. 8. La virgen. 9. El inglés. 10. El día. 11. La parte. 12. El teléfono.

23. NOUNS: USES • • • • • • • •

GRAMMAR

A. SPECIAL USES OF THE PLURAL. I. The plural of a masculine noun may represent two or more people, including both sexes:

(*a*) **Mis amigos.** My friends (all male or of both sexes).
(*b*) **Sus padres.** His parents.
(*c*) **Mis tíos.** My uncles (*or* my aunt and uncle *or* my aunts and uncles).

II. The plural of an abstract noun (or the singular used with the indefinite article) often expresses a concrete illustration of the abstraction. Thus, **locura** (insanity) becomes in the plural "mad deeds" or "mad thoughts":

(*a*) **Las locuras de don Quijote.** The mad deeds of Don Quixote.
(*b*) **Siempre dice muchos disparates.** He always makes many foolish remarks.
(*c*) **Por poco hago un disparate.** I almost did something foolish.

B. SPECIAL USE OF THE SINGULAR. When a singular notion is applicable to each one of a group, Spanish ordinarily uses a singular noun:

(*a*) **Los leones abrieron la boca.** The lions opened their mouths.
(*b*) **Los niños levantaron la mano.** The children raised their hands (each raised one hand).

C. USE OF PERSONAL **a** BEFORE THE NOUN. I. Before proper names of persons, and before other nouns denoting specific persons (i.e., those modified by a definite article, a possessive adjective, a demonstrative adjective) Spanish requires the preposition **a**. This **a** should not be translated; it serves merely to identify the direct object.

(*a*) **Hemos visto a Juan.** We have seen John.
(*b*) **Detuvieron al criminal.** They detained (arrested) the criminal.
(*c*) **Conocemos a su hermana.** We know his sister.
(*d*) **¿ Conoce Vd. a aquel hombre ?** Do you know that man ?

NOTE: The rule stated above applies to the personal object of most transitive verbs in Spanish. The student should remember, however, that some English transitive verbs must be translated into Spanish by a reflexive verb with a characteristic preposition other than **a**: I married Mary. **Me casé con María.** Do you remember Joe ? **¿ Se acuerda de Pepe ?** For other examples see Chap. 12, B.

II. Although this chapter deals with nouns, it is appropriate to emphasize here that all pronouns, too, which are used as the direct

[55]

object and refer to persons (except the unstressed **me, te, le,** etc.) are preceded by the preposition **a:**

(*a*) **Ella no vió a nadie.** She didn't see anybody.

(*b*) **Despidió a su secretaria y ahora busca a otra.** He fired his secretary and now he is looking for another.

III. Before nouns referring to animals which the speaker regards as having human attributes a personal **a** may be used:

Los niños querían mucho al perro de la familia. The children loved the family dog very much.

IV. When found before names of inanimate things, personal **a** indicates a tendency to personify the thing or to identify a direct object otherwise difficult to recognize:

(*a*) **Todos temen a la muerte.** All fear death.

(*b*) **A la guerra sigue la paz.** Peace follows war.

V. Before geographical proper nouns personal **a** may be used. (Students need not imitate this usage, since it seems to be disappearing from the language.)

Visitamos (a) París. We visited Paris.

EXERCISES

A. *Supply personal* a *where required, and give your reason for doing so:*
1. ¿ Dónde están nuestros amigos? No veo — ninguno. 2. ¿ Conoce Vd. — aquel hombre? 3. Llamó la Gaviota — su barco. 4. ¿ Recuerda Vd. — María Soledad? 5. Los pastores cuidaban — las ovejas. 6. ¿ Quién despertó — el gato? 7. Llamaron — el policía. 8. Vamos a elegir — un hombre que sepa gobernar. 9. Los niños no querían — su padre. 10. El ejército necesita — oficiales inteligentes.

B. *Translate to Spanish:* 1. The king and queen received the prime minister at noon. 2. The men took off their hats. 3. The students did not understand their professor. 4. The car overtook the truck. 5. She never speaks to anyone. 6. They notified Captain Jones. 7. I am looking for my dog. 8. My brother and sister flew to Miami.

24. PRONOUNS . . . .
SUBJECT & PREPOSITIONAL . . .

GRAMMAR

A. SUBJECT PRONOUNS.

yo		I	nosotros, –as		we
tú		you (*fam.*)	vosotros, –as		you (*fam.*)
usted	used with	you	ustedes	used with	you
él	3rd pers.	he	ellos	3rd pers.	they (*masc.*)
ella	of verb	she	ellas	of verb	they (*fem.*)

I. **Tú (hablas)** and **vosotros (habláis)** are used to address members of the family, intimate friends, and animals. **Usted (habla)** and **ustedes (hablan)** are used to address strangers and all persons regularly called by their last names.

II. Subject pronouns are used much less frequently in Spanish than in English. Those most frequently expressed are **usted, ustedes;** the one most rarely expressed is **vosotros.** In Spanish America **vosotros** is regularly replaced by **ustedes** (followed by the 3rd person plural of the verb).

III. Subject pronouns are most frequently expressed when there is a contrast of subjects:

(*a*) **Ella cosía mientras él fumaba.** She sewed while he smoked.
(*b*) **No lo dijo él sino ella.** He didn't say it but she did.

IV. Subject pronouns must be expressed in compound subjects:

Él y yo llegamos a las nueve. He and I arrived at nine.

V. Subject pronouns are used in translating the English phrases, "It is I (you, he, etc.)."

(*a*) **Soy yo.** It is I.
(*b*) **Somos nosotros.** It is we.

VI. Plural third person subject pronouns are expressed when modified by a noun in apposition; when similarly modified, first or second person pronouns may or may not be expressed:

(*a*) **Ustedes los americanos son optimistas.** You Americans are optimists.

(*b*) **(Nosotros) las mujeres somos así.** We women are like that.

B. Prepositional Pronouns.

(para) mí	(for) me	para nosotros, –as	for us
" ti (*fam.*)	" you	" vosotros, –as	" you
" usted	" you	" ustedes	" you
" él	" him, it	" ellos	" them
" ella	" her, it	" ellas	" them

Note: These forms are the same as the subject pronouns except for **mí** and **ti**. The reflexive form for the third person is **sí**.

I. The prepositional pronouns may be used with any preposition. **Con** combines with **mí, ti,** and **sí** to form **conmigo, contigo,** and **consigo.**

II. The prepositional pronouns are used with verbs that take a characteristic preposition before the object:

(*a*) **Soñó con ella.** He dreamed of her.

(*b*) **Juana no se acuerda de mí.** Jane doesn't remember me.

III. The prepositional pronouns are used to indicate the goal of motion (place or person):

Nos acercamos a ella. We approach her (*or* it).

IV. The prepositional pronouns are used in elliptical phrases involving such verbs as **faltar, gustar, parecer,** etc.:

¿ **Te parece bonita?** . . . **Pues, a mí tampoco.** Do you think she is pretty? Well, I don't either.

EXERCISES

A. *Indicate which of the italicized pronouns could be eliminated, and explain why you think the others should remain:* Yo *voy a la universidad todos los días.* Yo *llego a* ella *a las ocho y media, poco más o menos. Casi a la misma hora llegan mis amigos.* Ellos *son tres chicos madrileños.* Nosotros *los cuatro entramos a las nueve en la primera clase. Poco después entra en* ella *el profesor.* Él *y* yo *nos saludamos. Los otros suelen burlarse de* él. *A* él *no le hace gracia pero a* mí *sí.*

B. *Translate:* 1. You Frenchmen are more artistic than we Americans. 2. You (**usted**) and he have to obey the rules. 3. You (**tú**) and I will leave at once. 4. He used to read the paper while she prepared their dinner. 5. Who is it? It's he. 6. I like coffee, and so does he. 7. At the last moment she decided to go with me. 8. She can't remember his name. Do you remember it? 9. Who knocked on the door? It was (*pret.*) I.

25. PRONOUNS. . . . .

GRAMMAR

A. FORMS OF THE DIRECT OBJECT PRONOUNS

me	me	nos	us
te	you (*fam.*)	os	you (*fam.*)
le	him, you (*m.*)	los	them, you (*m.*)
lo	it (*m.*)		
la	her, you, it (*f.*)	las	them, you (*f.*)

NOTE: In certain parts of Spain, and generally in Spanish America, lo is commonly used to mean "him" as well as "it."

B. POSITION AND USES. I. The direct object pronouns precede the verb, except as noted in II and III;

(*a*) **Los vimos.** We saw them.
(*b*) **No lo digas.** Don't say it.

II. Direct object pronouns immediately follow affirmative commands, infinitives, and present participles. In writing, they are literally added to these forms, and a written accent is sometimes required to indicate that there has been no change of stress in the verb.

(*a*) **Hágalo Vd.** Do it.
(*b*) **Al advertirlo, eché a correr.** On noticing it, I began to run.
(*c*) **Mirándolo bien, uno puede descifrarlo.** By looking at it carefully, one can decipher it.

III. If an infinitive or present participle depends on an auxiliary verb, object pronouns are placed before the auxiliary or after the infinitive or present participle:

(*a*) **Estamos aprendiéndolo.**
   Lo estamos aprendiendo. } We are learning it.
(*b*) **Quiero comprarlos.**
   Los quiero comprar. } I want to buy them.

IV. When a direct object precedes the verb, it is commonly repeated by an object pronoun:

(a) **Al presidente yo le conocí en Cayo Hueso.** I met the president in Key West.
(b) **Eso no lo creemos.** We don't believe that.

V. The neuter direct object **lo** is used to represent a previously expressed idea:

(a) **Lo que Vd. dice es absurdo y no lo creo.** What you say is absurd and I don't believe it.
(b) **Él es rubio pero no lo es su prima.** He is blond but his cousin isn't.

EXERCISES

A. *Translate to English; then give the rule for the position of each object pronoun:* 1. No pudimos verlo claramente. 2. Al obispo Marroquín le querían mucho los indios. 3. Al pedirlo, se inclinó profundamente. 4. Ábrala Vd. 5. Viéndolos en la esquina, nos detuvimos un momento. 6. No lo repita Vd. delante de nadie. 7. Desde marzo le estamos esperando. 8. No lo puedo ver.

B. *Translate:* 1. My uncle is rich but I am not. 2. She told us what had happened but I don't believe it. 3. They were unable to put it (*refers to* **la luz**) out. 4. We tried to find you (*m. pl.*) all day. 5. I have seen her twice, but I have never seen him. 6. Their mother woke them (*f. pl.*) at seven o'clock. 7. Mr. Pérez [is the one] I met in Barcelona. 8. He cured his cold by going to bed early.

26. PRONOUNS . . . .

GRAMMAR

A. FORMS OF INDIRECT OBJECT PRONOUNS.

me	to me	**nos**	to us
te	to you (*fam.*)	**os**	to you (*fam.*)
le	to him, her, you, it	**les**	to them, you

B. POSITION AND USES.   I. Indirect object pronouns follow the same rules for position as the direct object pronouns.

II. When there are two object pronouns, the indirect precedes the direct:

Nos lo envió.   He sent it to us.

III. When both are third person, the indirect becomes **se:**

Se lo vendimos.   We sold it to him.

IV. Since **se** may represent either **le** or **les,** a prepositional pronoun is often needed for clarity:

Se lo vendimos a él (ella, usted, ellos, ellas, ustedes).   We sold it to him (her, you, them [*m. and f.*], you [*pl.*]).

V. Prepositional pronouns may be used for emphasis:

A mí no me gusta nada.   *I* don't like it at all.

VI. Indirect object pronouns are used frequently to indicate a person to whom the action or state expressed by a verb is of special interest.   Among the common notions expressed in this way are personal advantage (or disadvantage), possession, and separation:

(*a*) **Nos pintó la casa.**   He painted the house for us.
(*b*) **Le rompieron el brazo.**   They broke his arm.
(*c*) **Me quitó la cartera.**   He took my pocketbook away from me.
(*d*) **Le compré el auto.**   I bought the car from him.

• • • • • • • • INDIRECT OBJECT

EXERCISES

A. *Substitute object pronouns for the italicized nouns, and add the prepositional pronouns necessary for clarity.* MODEL: Enviamos *el baúl* a *la señora Pereda*. **Se lo enviamos a ella.** 1. Ofrecimos *el premio* a *José*. 2. Mandó *el paquete* a *su madre*. 3. Dirigieron *la carta* al *jefe*. 4. Robaron *las joyas* a *la actriz*. 5. Quitaron *los dulces* a *la niña*. 6. Vendieron *los libros* al *profesor*. 7. Contó *la historia* a su *hermana*. 8. Devolvieron *las sillas* al *fabricante*.

B. *Translate:* 1. He gave it (*refers to* **la carta**) to me. 2. They sent them (*refers to* **las naranjas**) to us. 3. She asked me for it (*refers to* **el libro**). 4. They buy coffee from us. 5. We will give them (*refers to* **los periódicos**) to you (*fam. sing.*). 6. He opened the door for us. 7. *She* didn't like it at all. 8. He seized my hand. 9. I'll sell it (*refers to* **la pluma**) to you.

27. POSSESSIVES · · · · · · · · ·

GRAMMAR

A. POSSESSIVE ADJECTIVES. There are two sets of possessive adjectives in Spanish, the unstressed and the stressed. The unstressed forms precede the noun and are the ones most frequently used. The stressed forms follow the noun (or **ser**) under the circumstances listed in **C, IV.**

UNSTRESSED FORMS

mi(s)	my	**nuestro(s), –a(s)**	our
tu(s)	your (*fam.*)	**vuestro(s), –a(s)**	your (*fam.*)
su(s)	his, her, your, its, their		

STRESSED FORMS

mío(s), –a(s)	my, of mine	**nuestro(s), –a(s)**	our, of ours
tuyo(s), –a(s)	your, of yours	**vuestro(s), –a(s)**	your, of yours
	suyo(s), –a(s)	his, of his; hers, of hers; etc.	

B. POSSESSIVE PRONOUNS. The possessive pronouns are formed by combining the stressed forms of the possessive adjectives with **el, la, los, las, lo: el mío, la mía, los míos, las mías,** etc.

C. USES OF THE POSSESSIVES. I. Possessive adjectives and pronouns agree in gender and number with the thing possessed, not (as in English) with the possessor. The adjectives are usually repeated before each noun they modify:

(*a*) **Mis libros y mis plumas.** My books and pens.
(*b*) ¿ **Han vuelto a su casa?** Have they returned to their house?
(*c*) **Nuestra casa y la suya.** Our house and theirs.

II. Since **su** has several meanings, clarity may require that it be replaced by the definite article with **de** + the proper prepositional pronoun:

Su casa = La casa de él (de ella, de usted, de ellos, de ellas, de ustedes). His (her, your, their) house.

[64]

III. The possessive pronouns may be clarified in the same manner:

El suyo = el de él (de ella, de usted, de ellos, etc.).

IV. The stressed forms of the possessive adjectives are used in direct address, after **ser,** and to translate the English phrases "of mine," "of yours," etc.

(a) **Ven acá, hijo mío.** Come here, my son.
(b) **Esta corbata es tuya.** This necktie is yours.
(c) **Pasamos el día con un amigo nuestro.** We spent the day with a friend of ours.

V. The masculine plural forms of the possessive pronouns are often used to express such ideas as "my men," "his folks," "our troops," etc.

(a) **Los nuestros avanzaron hacia el enemigo.** Our troops advanced toward the enemy.
(b) **El viejo cuidaba de los suyos.** The old man took care of his folks.

EXERCISES

A. *Supply the proper possessive adjective or pronoun:* 1. Ella se despidió de (*her*) novio. 2. Ese reloj es (*mine*). 3. Ayer conocí a un amigo (*of yours*, fam. sing.). 4. Su jardín es más grande que (*ours*). 5. Él se olvida de (*his*) viejos padres. 6. Todos (*their*) muebles son antiguos. 7. (*My*) tía y (*my*) primas viven juntas. 8. (*Our men*) atacaron con violencia. 9. Se presentó a las seis con un compañero (*of his*).

B. *Replace the italicized words with possessive pronouns.* 1. Hablamos con *sus padres*. 2. Juan perdió *su pluma*. 3. *Tu casa* es más nueva que *mi casa*. 4. *Tus flores* y *las de María*. 5. *Nuestras camisas* y *las de José*. 6. Nadie tiene un palacio como *vuestro palacio*. 7. Quiere Vd. buscar *mi sombrero* y *el de Pablo*. 8. Esta muchacha es *nuestra hija* y aquélla es *la de los vecinos*.

C. Which of the examples in EXERCISE B would not be clear as to the possessor if you failed to use prepositional pronouns for clarity? Restate the ambiguous examples showing how all possible meanings could be expressed.

28. DEMONSTRATIVES......

GRAMMAR

A. DEMONSTRATIVE ADJECTIVES.

	SINGULAR			PLURAL	
MASC.	FEM.		MASC.	FEM.	
este	esta	this	estos	estas	these
ese	esa	that	esos	esas	those
aquel	aquella	that	aquellos	aquellas	those

B. AGREEMENT AND USES OF DEMONSTRATIVE ADJECTIVES.

I. Demonstrative adjectives normally precede the nouns they modify. They agree with these nouns in gender and number and are usually repeated before each one:

Este papel, este lápiz, y esta pluma. This paper, pencil, and pen.

II. **Este** refers to persons, things, or events near the speaker in space or time. It corresponds to the adverbs **acá** and **aquí** (here):

(*a*) **Este cuadro que tengo aquí.** This picture which I have here.
(*b*) **Esta semana he hecho mucho.** This week I have done a lot.

III. **Ese** refers to persons, things, or events associated with the person spoken to. It corresponds to the adverb **ahí** (there):

(*a*) **Ese libro que tienes ahí.** That book which you have there.
(*b*) **Esa historia que cuentas es increíble.** That story which you tell is incredible.

IV. **Aquel** refers to persons, things, or events distant in space or time from both speaker and person spoken to. It corresponds to the adverbs **allá** and **allí** (there):

(*a*) **Aquel muchacho en la playa.** That boy on the beach.
(*b*) **En aquella época no había aviones.** At that time there were no airplanes.

C. DEMONSTRATIVE PRONOUNS. I. Demonstrative adjectives are changed to pronouns by the addition of a written accent on the stressed vowel (**éste, ése, aquél,** etc.). There are three neuter forms without written accent: **esto, eso, aquello.**

II. There is a fourth demonstrative pronoun identical in form with the definite article: **el, la, lo, los, las.**

[66]

D. Agreement and Uses of Demonstrative Pronouns.

I. Demonstrative pronouns agree in gender and number with the nouns they represent:

Nuestra casa y aquélla son nuevas. Our house and that one are new.

II. Demonstrative pronouns express exactly the same relationships in space and time as do demonstrative adjectives.

III. **Este,** etc. is used to indicate the second of two antecedents. It corresponds to English "the latter:"

Llegamos a la casa de Pedro cuando salía éste. We reached Peter's house when the latter was coming out.

NOTE: This use of **éste,** etc., alone is common. The forms of **éste** and **aquél** used together in the sense of "the latter" and "the former" are not common.

IV. The neuter forms **esto, eso,** and **aquello** are used to refer to an idea or to an object not yet identified. **Eso** is the most common of the three:

(*a*) **Eso es lo que dice todo el mundo.** That (what you have just said) is what everybody says.

(*b*) **¿ Qué es esto ? Es mi manta.** What is this? It's my blanket.

V. The pronouns **el, la, lo, los, las** are used before phrases introduced by **de** and before relative clauses (This last use is treated in Chap. 29):

(*a*) **Esperan la respuesta de Rusia y la del Japón.** They are waiting for Russia's reply and for Japan's (that of Japan).

(*b*) **El abogado de Juan y el de María son amigos.** John's lawyer and Mary's are friends.

(*c*) **Lo de las razas inferiores es una tontería.** That business of inferior races is nonsense.

(*d*) **Eso es lo de menos.** That's the least of it.

EXERCISES

A. *Translate the italicized words:* 1. ¿ De quién es (*that*) carta que acabas de recibir? 2. En (*those*) tiempos todo se escribía a mano. 3. (*That business*) del insulto fué una broma. 4. (*This*) muchacha es mi novia. 5. (*These*) árboles son más altos que (*those*) (across the river). 6. Mi familia y (*that*) de mi vecino. 7. Juan salió de su despacho y entró en (*that*) del jefe. 8. Juan y Pablo son mejicanos;

(*the latter*) acaba de llegar.   9. No nos fijamos en (*that*).   10. (*This*) es lo que quiero decir.

B. *Translate:*   1. That's it.   Now you are doing it right (**bien**). 2. This suit and necktie are new.   3. Bolívar's career resembles Washington's.   4. Where did you buy those shoes?   5. Who told you that?   6. Someone knocked on my door and on my brother's. 7. In those times men did not know how to read and write.   8. These trucks belong to Mr. Suárez.   9. That business of the senator is in all the newspapers.

29. RELATIVES . . . .

GRAMMAR

A. FORMS OF THE RELATIVE PRONOUNS.

que	that, which, who, whom
quien, quienes	who, whom, he who
el que, la que, los que, las que, lo que	he who, the one who *or* which; who, which
el cual, la cual, los cuales las cuales, lo cual	who, whom, that, which
cuanto, −a, −os, −as	as much as, all that (those)
cuyo, −a, −os, −as	whose, of which
donde	where, in which

B. AGREEMENT. Que and **donde** are invariable; **quien** agrees in number with its antecedent; all others agree with their antecedents in gender and number.

C. USES. I. SUBJECT OF VERB. Que is by far the most common relative pronoun. It may refer to both persons and things and introduce both restrictive and nonrestrictive clauses *:

(a) **El sombrero que está en la mesa.** The hat which is on the table.

(b) **La mujer que llegó ayer es mi madre.** The woman who arrived yesterday is my mother.

(c) **Mi mujer, que llegó ayer, está enferma.** My wife, who arrived yesterday, is sick.

II. OBJECT OF VERB. In this function also **que** is the pronoun most frequently used. It refers to both persons and things. The relative pronoun should not be omitted as its English equivalent sometimes is.

(a) **El reloj que compró Vd.** The watch [which] you bought.

(b) **La señorita que (a quien) vimos anoche.** The young lady [whom] we saw last night.

III. OBJECT OF A PREPOSITION. Referring to people, **quien** and **el que** are both common. **Quien** is more frequent after prepositions of one syllable. Referring to things, **que** is usual after **a, con, de, en; el cual,** after other prepositions.

---

* A restrictive clause is one that is needed to identify or define the antecedent (see examples **a** and **b** under **C,** I). A nonrestrictive clause is not needed to identify the antecedent; it merely adds incidental information (see example **c** under **C,** I).

(*a*) **El hombre con quien vine.** The man with whom I came.

(*b*) **Nos saludaron las chicas delante de las que nos habíamos sentado.** The girls in front of whom we had sat down greeted us.

(*c*) **Ésta es la casa en que (donde) vivimos.** This is the house in which we live.

(*d*) **Ésa es la tendencia contra la cual hay que luchar.** That is the tendency against which it is necessary to fight.

IV. **El cual** is often used to avoid confusion of antecedent. It indicates the more distant of two possible antecedents. When the antecedent is a previously expressed idea, the neuter **lo cual** is used.

(*a*) **Visitamos la catedral de Burgos, la cual contiene la tumba del Cid.** We visited the Burgos cathedral, which contains the tomb of the Cid.

(*b*) **El alcalde se negó a recibirle, lo cual nos enfadó a todos.** The mayor refused to receive him, which irritated all of us.

V. **Cuyo** is a possessive relative adjective. It may refer to either persons or things.

Ella se casó con el muchacho cuyo padre había sido juez. She married the boy whose father had been a judge.

VI. **El que** is the most frequently used compound relative (one involving its own antecedent). The neuter **lo que** translates English "what" (that which).

(*a*) **La que Vd. dice es la historia más famosa de la Edad Media.** The one you say is the most famous story of the Middle Ages.

(*b*) **El que (quien) trabaja, adelanta.** He who works, gets ahead.

(*c*) **Los que pudimos oírle aplaudimos.** Those of us who managed to hear him applauded.

(*d*) **Nos contó lo que había sucedido.** He told us what had happened.

VII. As a pronoun, **cuanto** involves its own antecedent; it is also used as a relative adjective.

(*a*) **Cuanto (todo lo que) Vd. dice me parece verdad.** Everything you say seems true to me.

(*b*) **Compró cuantas tierras pudo (todas las tierras que pudo).** He bought all the lands he could.

EXERCISES

A. *Supply the proper relative:* 1. Ésta es la frase (*whose*) sentido no comprendemos. 2. Déme Vd. ese libro y (*those which*) están en la mesa. 3. La playa (*which*) preferimos es ésta. 4. El muchacho (*who*) ganó el premio desapareció. 5. La cantante (*whom*) oyeron anoche es brasileña. 6. El señor González es el profesor con (*whom*) hice el viaje. 7. Allí está la fuente alrededor de (*which*) jugábamos. 8. Salió sin decir palabra, (*which*) nos extrañó. 9. Visitamos la isla en (*which*) había muerto el poeta. 10. El dinero (*which*) está en el cajón es mío.

B. *Translate:* 1. This park is beautiful but the one which we saw last week is more beautiful. 2. The president, who intends to spend two days in New York, has consented to speak. 3. In Lima they met their friend's daughter, who is very pretty. 4. He always advises those who seek advice. 5. Mr. Douglas is the man for whom I shall vote.

30. INTERROGATIVES ● ● ● ● ● ●

GRAMMAR

A. Questions. (*Note punctuation.*) I. ¿ **Quién**?, ¿ **quiénes**? *who?* refers only to persons. *Whom?* is translated ¿ **a quién**? and *whose?*, ¿ **de quién**?

(*a*) ¿ **Quién es aquel hombre**? Who is that man?
(*b*) ¿ **A quién conoció Vd. anoche**? Whom did you meet last night?
(*c*) ¿ **De quién es este auto**? Whose car is this?

Note: **De quién** must precede **ser**, not the noun as in English.

II. ¿ **Qué**? *what?* is both pronoun and adjective. It asks for definition when followed directly by **ser** + noun.

(*a*) ¿ **Qué son las Naciones Unidas**? What are the United Nations?
(*b*) ¿ **Qué es eso**? What is that?
(*c*) ¿ **En qué cine vió Vd. la película**? At what movie did you see the film?

III. ¿ **Cuál**?, ¿ **cuáles**? *which* (*one* or *ones*)? *what?* is commonly used only as pronoun. It implies selection rather than definition.

(*a*) ¿ **Cuál es su sobrino**? Which one is your nephew?
(*b*) ¿ **Cuál es la lección para mañana**? What is the lesson for tomorrow?

IV. ¿ **Cómo**? *how?* usually implies manner or condition. Followed by **ser** it asks for description. It is often used in the sense of *what* (*did you say*)? or *what* (*do you mean*)?

(*a*) ¿ **Cómo está su novia**? How is your sweetheart?
(*b*) ¿ **Cómo es su novia**? What is your sweetheart like?
(*c*) ¿ **Cómo dijo Vd.**? What did you say?
(*d*) ¿ **Es éste el pueblo de Vd.**? ¿ **Cómo pueblo**? Is this your town? What do you mean "town"?

V. ¿ **Cuánto** (**–a, –os, –as**)? *how much? how many?* is both adjective and pronoun.

(*a*) ¿ **Cuánto compró Vd.**? How much did you buy?
(*b*) ¿ **Cuántos años pasaron en el Brasil**? How many years did they spend in Brazil?

VI. ¿ **Qué tal**? *how?* frequently asks for evaluation or opinion. It is often used alone as a greeting.

[72]

(a) ¿ Qué tal es el coche nuevo ? How is the new car ?
(b) ¿ Qué tal están los caminos ? How are the roads ?
(c) Hola, María, ¿ qué tal ? Hello, Mary, how goes it ?

B. EXCLAMATIONS. I. ¡ Qué ! is used to translate *how!* before adjectives and adverbs and to translate *what!* or *what a!* before nouns. If the noun is modified, the adjective follows the noun preceded by **tan** or **más.**

(a) ¡ Qué hermoso ! How beautiful !
(b) ¡ Qué lástima ! What a pity !
(c) ¡ Qué inteligencia muestra ! What intelligence he shows !
(d) ¡ Qué noche tan serena ! What a calm night !

II. ¡ Cuánto ! is used to translate *how!* before verbs and *how!* or *how much (many)!* before nouns.

(a) ¡ Cuánto lo siento ! How sorry I am !
(b) ¡ Cuántos días alegres pasamos en España ! How many happy days we spent in Spain !

EXERCISES

A. *Translate the italicized words:* 1. ¿ (*Who*) es aquella señorita ? 2. ¿ (*What*) es aquella señorita ? 3. ¿ (*Which*) señorita quiere Vd. decir ? 4. ¿ A (*which*) de las dos se refiere Vd. ? 5. ¡ (*What a*) tontería ! 6. ¿ (*What*) es el número de su casa ? 7. ¿ Con (*whom*) fué ella al cine ? 8. ¿ (*What*) es la zoología ? 9. ¡ (*How*) nos extrañó su ausencia ! 10. ¿ (*What*) es eso ?

B. *Translate:* 1. How is your Mexican friend ? 2. What is he like ? 3. How is the road to (**de**) Mexico ? 4. Is this girl your sister ? — What do you mean "sister" ? She's my wife. 5. On what boat did you go to Cuba ? 6. Which is the boat you went on ? 7. To whom did you send the telegram ? 8. Whose necktie is that ?

31. NEGATIVES & INDEFINITES .

GRAMMAR

A. Verbs are made negative by placing **no** or some other negative word before them. Only object pronouns may stand between a negative and the verb:

(*a*) **No tengo dinero.** I have no money.
(*b*) **Nunca sales sin paraguas.** You never go out without an umbrella.
(*c*) **No se lo vendí.** I didn't sell it to him.

B. Memorize the following list of negative words and note in illustrative sentences that **no** must be used before the verb no matter how many negatives follow it. **No** is not needed with a negative word that stands alone.

nadie	nobody, not . . . anybody
nada	nothing, not . . . anything
ninguno (ningún)	not one, no one
nunca ⎫ **jamás** ⎭	never, not ever
tampoco	neither, not either
ni . . . ni	neither . . . nor

(*a*) **Nadie sabe lo que pasó.** Nobody knows what happened.
(*b*) **No he dicho nunca nada a nadie.** I have never told anybody anything.
(*c*) **¿ Qué dice Vd.?** — **Nada.** What are you saying? Nothing.
(*d*) **No conozco a ningún abogado.** — **Yo tampoco.** I don't know any lawyer. Neither do I.

NOTE: **Alguno** may replace **ninguno** as a strong negative adjective. When so used it always follows the noun: **No conozco a abogado alguno.** I don't know any lawyer (whatsoever).

(*e*) **Ni Juan ni María * han venido hoy.** Neither John nor Mary has come today.

C. Jámas (or **alguna vez**) is used to translate "ever" in questions without negative implication:

¿ Ha visto Vd. jamás el pico de Orizaba? Have you ever seen Orizaba peak ?

* Unlike their English equivalents, **ni . . . ni** usually take a plural verb in Spanish.

[74]

D. Negatives are used after **sin** (**sin que**) and after comparatives:

(*a*) **Se fué sin despedirse de nadie.** He left without taking leave of anybody.
(*b*) **Entró sin que nadie le viera.** He entered without anybody seeing him.
(*c*) **Ahora canta ella mejor que nunca.** Now she sings better than ever.

NOTE: A good way for an English-speaking student to assure himself that a negative word is correct in Spanish is to formulate a question about the statement to be translated. Applying this suggestion to the last two examples of **D**, we would say of the first, "Who saw him enter?" The answer is clearly *nobody*. Therefore Spanish uses **nadie**. The second question would be, "When did she sing better?" And the answer, *never;* hence, **nunca**.

E. The affirmative equivalents of **nadie, nada,** and **ninguno** are **alguien, algo,** and **alguno**. They should be used to translate *somebody, something,* and *some* or *any* when it is clear that these are not used merely to avoid a double negative (as in "I haven't seen anybody"):

(*a*) **Alguien nos está siguiendo.** Somebody is following us.
(*b*) ¿ **Qué es eso? Algo misterioso.** What is that? Something mysterious.

F. Algo and **nada** are often used as adverbs:

(*a*) **La historia es algo complicada.** The story is a bit complicated.
(*b*) **Ella no es nada simpática.** She isn't at all nice.

EXERCISES

A. *Translate the following Spanish sentences into English, noting especially how often the italicized negative may be translated by an affirmative in English:* 1. *Nadie* sabe quién es el autor de « Lazarillo de Tormes ». 2. No le he visto salir con *nadie*. 3. No hay *nada* más interesante que la ciencia. 4. *Nunca* he estudiado *nada* tan interesante. 5. Pues, a mí no me parece *nada* interesante. 6. No le gusta a Juan *ninguno* de estos libros. *Ni* a mí *tampoco*. 7. *Ninguno* de mis amigos ha podido enterarse de la verdad. 8. No hemos realizado ganancia *alguna*.

B. *Translate:* 1. He never gives anything to anybody. 2. Who has just sat down? Nobody. 3. Have you ever been in Havana? 4. He entered the room without greeting anybody. 5. Mr. Casals plays the cello better than anybody. 6. Music doesn't interest me at all. 7. I know somebody who can help you. 8. She is very intelligent but somewhat homely.

32. ADJECTIVES: PART I . . . . .

GRAMMAR

A. INFLECTION OF ADJECTIVES. I. Adjectives form their plurals in the same way as nouns (see Chap. 22).

II. Adjectives which end in –o change o to a to form the feminine; all other adjectives have identical forms for masculine and feminine except as noted in (1) and (2):

(1) Adjectives of nationality ending in a consonant add **a** to form the feminine: **inglés, inglesa; alemán, alemana.**

(2) Adjectives ending in –**án**, –**ón**, –**or** add **a** to form the feminine: **holgazán, holgazana** (*lazy*); **preguntón, preguntona** (*inquisitive*); **hablador, habladora** (*talkative*).

NOTE: Adjectives derived from Latin comparatives do not change in the feminine: **inferior, superior, mejor, mayor,** etc.

B. AGREEMENT OF ADJECTIVES. Adjectives agree in gender and number with the nouns they modify:

Libros rojos y plumas negras. Red books and black pens.

C. APOCOPATION OF ADJECTIVES. I. The following adjectives regularly drop final o before a masculine singular noun: **alguno, bueno, malo, ninguno, primero, tercero.** In their shortened form **alguno** and **ninguno** take a written accent: **algún libro, ningún hombre.**

II. **Grande** may become **gran** before a singular noun of either gender:

(*a*) **Una gran poetisa.** A great poetess.
(*b*) **Un gran poeta.** A great poet.

III. **Santo** becomes **San** before the names of masculine saints except those beginning with **To–** or **Do–:**

(*a*) **San José.** Saint Joseph.
(*b*) **Santo Tomás.** Saint Thomas.

D. COMPARISON OF ADJECTIVES. Three kinds of comparison are possible: *inferiority, superiority,* and *equality.*

I. The comparative of inferiority is regularly formed by putting **menos** before the adjective: **rico, menos rico:** *rich, less rich.*

II. The comparative of superiority is formed regularly by putting **más** before the adjective: **rico, más rico:** *rich, richer.*

In Spanish no distinction is made between the *higher* degree of two individuals and the *highest* degree of three or more, that is to say, there is no specific form for expressing a superlative. In translating comparatives and superlatives from English to Spanish it is usually safe to use the definite article in Spanish whenever it is expressed in English. Note the following examples:

(a) *John and Peter are brothers.* Peter is the taller.   *Juan y Pedro son hermanos.* **Pedro es el más alto.**

(b) *John, Paul, and Peter are friends.* Peter is the tallest.   *Juan, Pablo, y Pedro son amigos.* **Pedro es el más alto.**

III. Five common adjectives are compared irregularly:

mucho, más	much, more
bueno, mejor	good, better
malo, peor	bad, worse
grande, mayor	large, larger (old, older)
pequeño, menor	small, smaller (young, younger)

Grande and **pequeño** may also be compared regularly. The regular forms usually refer to size; the irregular, to the age of persons.

(a) **El libro más grande.** The largest book.
(b) **Mi hijo mayor.** My oldest son.

IV. English "in" after a superlative is translated **de:**

El hombre más distinguido del pueblo. The most distinguished man in the town.

V. "Than" is regularly expressed by **que** except before numerals or expressions implying number. In these cases **de** is used:

(a) **Juan es más alto que José.** John is taller than Joseph.
(b) **Gastó más de cien dólares.** He spent more than a hundred dollars.
(c) **Gastó más de la mitad de su dinero.** He spent more than half of his money.

NOTE: Occasionally other formulas are needed to translate "than." When the "than" clause contains a finite verb, "than" is translated **de lo que** or **del que, de la que, de los que, de las que. De lo que** is used when comparison is made with an idea expressed in the main clause by an adjective or adverb:

Los problemas son más graves de lo que creíamos. The problems are graver than we thought (they were grave).

The inflected forms are used when comparison is made with a specific noun in the main clause:

Los rusos tienen más problemas de los que tenemos nosotros. The Russians have more problems than we have (problems).

VI. Comparisons of equality are expressed by **tan . . . como** if the term of comparison is stated; by **tan** alone, if it is not. Quantitative comparisons of equality are expressed by **tanto, –a, –os, –as . . . como**:

(*a*) **Él es tan inteligente como ella.** He is as intelligent as she.
(*b*) **Me alegro que sean Vds. tan puntuales.** I am glad you are so punctual.
(*c*) **Vd. tiene tanto tiempo como yo.** You have as much time as I do.

VII. The ending **–ísimo** is added to the stem of adjectives to express a high degree of a quality without any sense of comparison:

(*a*) **Una mujer hermosísima.** A very beautiful woman.
(*b*) **Un hombre riquísimo.** An extremely wealthy man.

EXERCISES

A. *Change the italicized word to agree with the noun it modifies, if it does not agree as it stands:* 1. Un hombre *socialista.* 2. La parte *inferior.* 3. Dos muchachas *encantador.* 4. Una mujer *francés.* 5. Una niña *cortés.* 6. Una cocinera *andaluz.* 7. Una alumna *feliz.* 8. Las reglas *general.* 9. Unos pícaros *burlón.* 10. Una criada *torpe.*

B. *Translate:* 1. A good friend. 2. A great actress. 3. The third chapter. 4. Some day. 5. Saint Dominic. 6. His youngest son is three years old. 7. John is stronger than Paul. 8. He is the strongest boy in the class. 9. He can lift more than two hundred pounds. 10. Of the two brothers John is the more intelligent.

33. ADJECTIVES: PART II . . . .

GRAMMAR

A. POSITION OF ADJECTIVES. Adjectives may be divided into two classes: *limiting* and *qualifying*. Limiting adjectives restrict the application of a noun or other substantive. Qualifying adjectives distinguish a substantive from others of its class or add a description of appearance, character, or value.

I. Among the limiting adjectives are the articles; the indefinite, negative, demonstrative, interrogative, possessive, and relative adjectives; and the numerals. Normally they precede the nouns they modify: **Ese libro, ningún libro, ¿ qué libro ?, tres libros,** etc.

II. Qualifying adjectives may precede or follow the nouns they modify. Some of the commonest adjectives usually precede the noun: **bueno, malo, grande.**

III. A qualifying adjective follows the noun it modifies when it serves to distinguish that noun from others of its class. Adjectives most likely to be used in this way are those of color, size, form, those derived from proper nouns, and past participles:

(*a*) **Una casa blanca.**   A white house (*not a brown or red one*).
(*b*) **Una mesa redonda.**   A round table (*not a square one*).
(*c*) **Un escritor mejicano.**   A Mexican writer.
(*d*) **Una carta firmada.**   A signed letter.

IV. A qualifying adjective normally precedes the noun it modifies when it expresses a quality already associated with that noun or adds a description not essential to our recognition of it:

(*a*) **La Santa Virgen.**   The Holy Virgin.
(*b*) **El fiero tigre.**   The fierce tiger.
(*c*) **El famoso pintor.**   The famous painter (*one whose fame has already been mentioned or is taken for granted*).

V. Two descriptive adjectives which modify the same noun may usually be placed without difficulty according to the rules already stated. However, the following added suggestions may prove helpful: If both adjectives precede or follow the noun they are connected by **y,** unless one of them is associated with the noun almost as a single concept. The adjective thus closely associated is always placed immediately after the noun.

(*a*) **Las estrechas y tortuosas calles de Sevilla.** The narrow, winding streets of Seville.

(*b*) **Una mujer alta y delgada.** A tall, slender woman.

(*c*) **Un hermoso caballo árabe.** A beautiful Arabian horse.

(*d*) **Poetas españoles contemporáneos.** Contemporary Spanish poets.

VI. The meaning of certain adjectives varies sharply according to their position. In their more literal, objective meaning they follow the noun:

un gran hombre, a great man	**un hombre grande,** a large man
un pobre hombre (to be pitied)	**un hombre pobre** (indigent)
el mismo hombre, the same man	**el hombre mismo,** the man himself
un nuevo traje, a different suit	**un traje nuevo,** a new suit

B. ADJECTIVES USED AS NOUNS. I. Adjectives (and past participles) are used as nouns with great frequency in Spanish:

(*a*) **El viejo y el joven.** The old man and the young man.

(*b*) **Los vivos y los muertos.** The living and the dead.

II. The neuter article **lo** is often placed before an adjective or past participle to form a kind of abstract noun:

(*a*) **Lo bello.** The beautiful.

(*b*) **Lo hecho.** That which (what) is done.

(*c*) **Lo peor es . . .** The worst of it is . . .

EXERCISES

Translate: 1. Cervantes wrote the first modern novel. 2. This famous writer lived a heroic life. 3. He took part in many celebrated battles. 4. From Granada one can see the white snow of the Sierra Nevada. 5. The best part of it is that I have no classes on Saturdays. 6. He bought a good Mexican saddle. 7. Columbus himself did not realize that he had discovered the New World. 8. This is the same lesson we studied yesterday. 9. In spite of his money the poor man is not happy. 10. They have just rented a large, comfortable house. 11. Old people (*don't translate "people"*) often cannot find employment.

[80]

34. ADVERBS . . . . •

GRAMMAR

A. SIMPLE ADVERBS. There are dozens of very common simple adverbs, which should be learned as met (**aquí, ahora, acaso,** etc.).

I. The most common simple adverb is **ya.** Used with the present tense, it means "now" or "already"; with past tenses, "already" or "just"; with future tenses, "presently" or "later".

(*a*) ¿ **Dónde está su amigo?** — **Ya viene.** Where is your friend? He is coming now.
(*b*) **Ya está aquí.** He is already here.
(*c*) **Ya lo he hecho.** I have already done it.
(*d*) **Ya llegó el tren.** The train has just arrived.

NOTE: Sometimes **ya** gives the preterite the value of a present perfect.

(*e*) **Ya nos veremos.** We'll see each other later.

B. ADVERBS OF MANNER. These are formed by adding **–mente** to the feminine singular of adjectives. If the adjective bears a written accent, the accent is retained in the adverb. If two such adverbs are joined by a conjunction, **–mente** is added only to the second:

lento, slow   **lentamente,** slowly
rápido, rapid   **rápidamente,** rapidly
lenta y cuidadosamente, slowly and carefully

C. ADVERBIAL PHRASES. Adverbial phrases are employed frequently in place of adverbs in **–mente:**

(*a*) **Trabaja con cuidado.** He works carefully.
(*b*) **Se portó de una manera extraña.** He behaved strangely.

D. POSITION OF ADVERBS. Adverbs normally precede the adjectives or adverbs they modify. Adverbs modifying verbs normally are placed directly before or after them:

(*a*) **Es muy bonita.** She is very pretty.
(*b*) **Canta muy bien.** She sings very well.
(*c*) **Pronto acabaremos.** We will soon finish.
(*d*) **Pedro andaba despacio.** Peter was walking slowly.

E. COMPARISON OF ADVERBS. I. Comparison of equality is expressed by **tan ... como**; comparison of superiority or inferiority, by **más ... que** or **menos ... que**:

(*a*) **Aprende tan despacio como yo.** He learns as slowly as I.
(*b*) **No coma Vd. tan de prisa.** Don't eat so fast.
(*c*) **Se acuesta más temprano que las gallinas.** He goes to bed earlier than the chickens.
(*d*) **Ahora viene más a menudo.** Now he comes more often.
(*e*) **Parece menos triste que antes.** He seems less sad than before.

NOTE: The term of comparison is often omitted as in (*b*) and (*d*).

II. IRREGULAR COMPARATIVES:

bien, well	**mejor,** better	**mucho,** much	**más,** more
mal, badly	**peor,** worse	**poco,** little	**menos,** less

III. SUPERLATIVE. There is no regular form to indicate the superlative. Context will often give superlative force to a comparative form. (Cf. Chapter 32, **D.**) Compare the following examples:

(*a*) **Este libro me gusta más que ése.** I like this book better than that one.
(*b*) **De todos los libros que he leído me gusta más éste.** Of all the books I have read I like this one most.

IV. A device which in some cases may be used to express the superlative is **lo más ... posible**:

Los niños se escaparon de la escuela lo más pronto posible. The children escaped from school as soon as possible.

EXERCISES

Translate: 1. We go to the movies very frequently (*two ways*). 2. I used to play the piano as well as she. 3. Now she plays much better than I. 4. My wife will be back presently. 5. Come back as soon as possible. 6. Our maid always disappears when we need her most. 7. Mary swims effortlessly. 8. The artist was painting slowly and patiently. 9. I like both houses, but I believe I like this one better. 10. My cousin already knows how to speak Spanish.

35. PREPOSITIONS . . . .

GRAMMAR

The many Spanish prepositions and their uses cannot be summarized in a brief chapter, and must be learned as met. The prepositions **por** and **para** are, however, of prime importance and require special attention. (For prepositions with infinitives, see Chap. 10.)

A. THE PREPOSITION **para.** I. **Para** is in large measure a *forward-looking* preposition. Thus, it expresses (1) destination (for), (2) purpose (to, in order to), (3) intended use or suitability (for), (4) limit of time (for, by):

1(*a*) **Mañana salgo para Miami.** Tomorrow I leave for Miami.
1(*b*) **Esta carta es para usted.** This letter is for you.
2(*a*) **Te escribo para invitarte a pasar unos días con nosotros.** I am writing you to invite you to spend a few days with us.
2(*b*) **Mi hijo estudia para abogado.** My son is studying for the law (to be a lawyer).
3(*a*) **Un vaso para agua.** A water glass.
3(*b*) **Pepe no es bueno para nada.** Joe is good for nothing.
4(*a*) **Para mañana lean Vds. el capítulo siguiente.** For tomorrow read the following chapter.
4(*b*) **Tendrán que terminarlo para el otoño.** They will have to finish it by autumn.

II. **Para** expresses personal point of view and relation to a standard:

(*a*) **Para mí el dinero tiene poca importancia.** For me money has little importance.
(*b*) **Para niño sabe mucho.** He knows a lot for a child.
(*c*) **Para lo que viene, esto no es nada.** Compared with what is coming, this is nothing.

III. **Estar para** + infinitive means "to be about to", with a noun it means "to be in the mood for".

(*a*) **Estábamos para acostarnos.** We were about to go to bed.
(*b*) **No está para bromas.** He is in no mood for jokes.

B. Por. I. **Por** expresses passage through time or space. It may also indicate vague time or place:

(*a*) **El banco quedó cerrado por tres días.** The bank remained closed for three days.
(*b*) **Entró por la puerta trasera.** He entered by the back door.

(c) **Solía pasear por la Quinta Avenida.** He used to stroll along Fifth Avenue.

(d) **Eso occurió por el año de 1937.** That happened around the year 1937.

(e) **Por aquí no hay cafés.** There are no cafés around here.

II. **Por** may express (1) agency, (2) means, (3) motive, (4) exchange, (5) measure, and (6) rate:

1. **América fué descubierta por Colón.** America was discovered by Columbus.
2. **Mandó la carta por avión.** He sent the letter by airmail.
3(a) **Por modestia no dice nada.** Out of modesty he says nothing.
3(b) **Lo hizo por molestarlos.** He did it to bother them (**para** could also be used, but **por** stresses motive).
4. **Le dí dos dólares por el libro.** I gave him two dollars for the book.
5. **En España se vende la leche por litros.** In Spain milk is sold by the liter.
6. **Cincuenta millas por hora.** Fifty miles an hour.

III. **Por** is used to translate "for (the sake of)", "in behalf of", "by" and "for" in oaths and exclamations:

(a) **Lo hizo por su vieja madre.** He did it for his old mother.
(b) **Habló por el bien de la República.** He spoke for the good of the country.
(c) **¡Por Dios!** For Heaven's sake!

IV. Before infinitives **por** often indicates action yet to be finished:

Me quedan veinte páginas por leer. I have twenty pages left to read.

V. **Estar por** means "to stand for" or "be in favor of":

Estoy por ir al cine. I'm in favor of going to the movies.

VI. After certain verbs (**ir, venir, mandar**) **por** indicates the object of an errand:

Vino por el coche. He came for the car.

EXERCISES

Supply **para** *or* **por** *for each blank, and translate into English:* 1. El hombre necesita poco — ser feliz. 2. Tenía la cara quemada — el sol. 3. Los domingos eran días felices — mí. 4. Vendió su automóvil — unos mil dólares. 5. La lluvia entraba en la sala — la ventana abierta. 6. Su padre le llevó — la senda hasta la orilla del lago. 7. Aquellas casitas sirven — guardar el maíz. 8. He comprado este magnífico regalo — ti. 9. A las siete saldremos — la estación. 10. — mujer es muy fuerte. 11. Me encaminé al bosque para llamar al perro, pero no aparecía — allí. 12. — el sábado tenemos que entregar un tema escrito. 13. — largos años vivió en aquel valle remoto. 14. Las mercancías deben mandarse — camión. 15. Cuando nosotros llegamos nuestro amigo ya estaba — marcharse. 16. El senador había tenido tantos disgustos que estaba — abandonar la política. 17. Tengo que comprar un cepillo — los dientes. 18. — el mes de diciembre cayó enfermo su padre. 19. Los indios nos llamaron — señas. 20. Muchos héroes se han sacrificado — su patria. 21. Se alquilan los autos — horas o — días. 22. Mi madre me mandó — el médico. 23. Le quedan — escribir sólo dos capítulos de su libro.

36. WORD ORDER . . . .

GRAMMAR

A. DECLARATIVE SENTENCES. In Spanish the subject tends to follow the verb under these conditions (1) when otherwise the sentence would end with a finite verb, (2) when the sentence begins with an adverb or adverbial phrase, (3) when the subject has a lengthy modifier (particularly a relative clause), (4) with verbs of saying, asking, and the like after a direct quotation, (5) in dependent clauses:

1(*a*) **Ha llegado mi primo.** My cousin has arrived.
1(*b*) **Se alquilan cuartos.** Rooms for rent.
1(*c*) **Me faltan dos botones.** Two of my buttons are missing.

2(*a*) **Pronto huyeron los ladrones.** The thieves soon fled.
2(*b*) **En esta casa vive una mejicana.** A Mexican woman lives in this house.

3. **Ha desaparecido el perro que compré ayer.** The dog I bought yesterday has disappeared.
4. **¿ Cómo está su mamá ? — preguntó Juan.** "How old is your mother?" asked John.
5. **Éste es el cuarto donde murió el poeta.** This is the room where the poet died.

B. QUESTIONS. I. Interrogative words always stand first in questions:

¿ Quién descubrió la penicilina ? Who discovered penicillin?

II. In questions, noun or pronoun subjects follow the verb:

¿ Se ha levantado su padre ? Has your father gotten up?

III. In questions, if the predicate contains a short adverb, object, predicate adjective or noun, the subject usually follows it:

(*a*) **¿ Ocurrió ayer el accidente ?** Did the accident occur yesterday?
(*b*) **¿ Vieron la película sus amigos ?** Did your friends see the picture?
(*c*) **¿ Está malo su marido ?** Is your husband sick?
(*d*) **¿ Es de oro ese reloj ?** Is that watch gold?

EXERCISES

Translate: 1. Are your parents at home? 2. Cigarettes are sold everywhere. 3. The book which you gave me interests me very much.   4. This is the town in which Lincoln used to work.   5. Did the president sign the law ?   6. Three years later the key which he had lost was found.   7. Do you think this hat becomes me ?   8. At that moment a shout was heard.   9. This morning the cook left.   10. "This is the road to Toledo," John said.

VOCABULARIES

ABBREVIATIONS

adj.	adjective	*n.*	noun
adv.	adverb	*neut.*	neuter
art.	article	*obj.*	object
conj.	conjunction	*pers.*	personal
def.	definite	*pl.*	plural
dem.	demonstrative	*p.p.*	past participle
dir.	direct	*prep.*	preposition or prepositional
f.	feminine	*pron.*	pronoun
fam.	familiar	*refl.*	reflexive
indef.	indefinite	*rel.*	relative
indir.	indirect	*Sp.*	Spanish
inf.	infinitive	*subj.*	subject
m.	masculine		

Spanish-English Vocabulary

In this vocabulary the chapter treating each irregular verb is indicated by printing the number of the chapter after the infinitive: **andar 3.**

A

a to, at
abandonar to abandon
abogado *m.* lawyer
abrir (*p.p.* **abierto**) to open
abstracción *f.* abstraction
absurdo, –a absurd
abuelo *m.* grandfather
acá here, over here
acabar to finish, end; — **de** + *inf.* to have just
acaso perhaps
accidente *m.* accident
acentuar 7 (**ú**) to accentuate
acercarse 6 (**a**) to approach, draw near (to)
aconsejar to advise
acordarse 5 (**ue**) (**de**) to remember
acostar 5 (**ue**) to put to bed; —**se** to go to bed
actriz *f.* actress
actuar 7 (**ú**) to act
adelantar to advance, get ahead
adquirir 5 (**ie**) to acquire
advertir 5 (**ie, i**) to notice; to warn
aficionado, –a (**a**) fond (of); *n.* fan, devotee
afirmar to affirm, assert
agradecido, –a grateful
agua *f.* water
ahí there (*near the person spoken to*)
ahora now
alcalde *m.* mayor
alcanzar 6 to overtake, reach
alegrarse (**de**) to be glad (of); **alegrarse** (**de que**) to be glad (that)
alegre merry, happy
alemán *adj. and n.* German; *m.* German (*language*)
Alfonso Alphonso
algo something
alguien someone, somebody
alguno, –a some, any; *pron.* someone, anyone

alma *f.* soul; heart
alquilar to rent
alrededor de around
alto, –a high, tall
alumna *f.* pupil, student
alumno *m.* pupil, student
allá there (*less precise than* **allí**)
allí there
americano, –a American
amigo *m.* friend
Andalucía *f.* Andalusia (*southern part of Spain*)
andaluz, –a Andalusian
andar 3 to walk, go
animal *m.* animal
anoche last night
antes *adv.* before; *conj.* — (**de**) **que** before
antiguo, –a old, ancient
año *m.* year
aparecer 6 to appear
apartado, –a remote
aplaudir to applaud
aprender to learn
aquel *dem. adj.* that; **aquél** *dem. pron.* that (one)
aquello *neut. dem. pron.* that
aquí here
árabe Arabian
árbol *m.* tree
Argentina *f.* Argentina
arrancar 6 to pull out
arte *m. and f.* art
así thus, so, in this (that) way
asistir (**a**) to attend, be present (at)
asombroso, –a astonishing, amazing
asunto *m.* affair; subject
atacar 6 to attack
atreverse (**a**) to dare
atrevido, –a bold
aun even; **aún** yet, still
aunque although, even though
ausencia *f.* absence
auto *m.* car

automóvil *m.* automobile
autor *m.* author
avanzar 6 to advance
avenida *f.* avenue
averiguar 6 to ascertain, find out
avión *m.* airplane
ayer yesterday
ayudar (a) to help
azul blue

B

bailar to dance
banco *m.* bank
bandido *m.* bandit
bañar to bathe; —se to take a bath
barco *m.* boat
Baroja, Pío (1872–) *Sp. novelist*
baúl *m.* trunk
beber to drink
belleza *f.* beauty
bello, –a beautiful
bien *adv.* well; *n.* good
billete *m.* ticket
blanco, –a white
boca *f.* mouth
bondad *f.* kindness
bonito, –a pretty
bosque *m.* woods, forest
botón *m.* button
Brasil *m.* Brazil
brasileño, –a Brazilian
brazo *m.* arm
broma *f.* joke, jest
bueno, –a good
Burgos *m. city of Old Castile*
burlarse (de) to make fun (of)
burlón, –a mocking
buscar 6 to look for, seek

C

caballo *m.* horse
caber 3 to be contained, fit (into)
cada *adj.* each; — uno *pron.* each
(one)
caer 4 to fall
café *m.* coffee; café
cajón *m.* drawer

callado, –a silent
callar(se) to be silent, not answer
calle *f.* street
cama *f.* bed
cambiar to change; to exchange
caminante *m.* traveler
caminar to travel, walk
camino *m.* road, way
camión *m.* truck
Canadá *m.* Canada
cansado, –a tiresome
cantante *m. and f.* singer
cantar to sing
cántaro: llover a —s to pour
capítulo *m.* chapter
Carlos *m.* Charles
caro, –a dear, expensive
carretera *f.* highway
carta *f.* letter
cartera *f.* wallet, pocketbook
casa *f.* house; a — home; en — home,
at home
casarse (con) to marry
casi almost
caso *m.* case; hacer — de to pay attention to
catedral *f.* cathedral
Cayo Hueso *m.* Key West
cazar 6 to hunt
célebre celebrated, famous
cepillo *m.* brush
cerrar 5 (ie) to close
(el) Cid Ruy Díaz de Vivar *11th century Sp. hero*
cielo *m.* sky; heaven
ciencia *f.* science
ciento (cien) a hundred, one hundred
cierto, –a certain, sure; a certain
cigarrillo *m.* cigarette
cigarro *m.* cigar; cigarette
cine *m.* movie (theater)
ciudad *f.* city
claramente clearly
clase *f.* class
clima *m.* climate
cocinera *f.* cook
coche *m.* carriage; car
coger 6 to catch, seize
Colón Columbus

comenzar 6 (**ie**) (**a**) to begin, start
comer to eat
comerciante *m.* merchant
como as, like; — **si** as if
¿cómo? how? what?
compañero *m.* companion
complicado, –a complicated
comprar to buy
comprender to understand
con with
concluir 7 to conclude, finish
conde *m.* count, earl
conducir 4 to conduct, lead
conductor *m.* conductor
confiar 7 (**í**) to confide, entrust, trust
conmigo with me, with myself
conocer 6 to know, be acquainted with, make the acquaintance of
consentir 5 (**ie, i**) (**en**) to consent (to)
consigo with himself, herself, yourself, themselves
construir 7 to construct
contar 5 (**ue**) to count; to tell (*a story*)
contemporáneo, –a contemporary
contener 3 contain
contigo with you, yourself (*fam.*)
continuar 7 (**ú**) to continue, go on
contra against
convenir 3 to be proper, be advisable
corbata *f.* necktie
correr to run
corrida *f.* bullfight
cortés courteous
cosa *f.* thing
coser to sew
crecer 6 to grow
creer 7 to believe, think
criada *f.* servant, maid
criminal *m.* criminal
cruel cruel
cruzar 6 to cross
cuadro *m.* picture
cual: el —, la —, *etc.* which
¿cuál? which (one)? what?
cualquier(a) *adj.* any (at all), whatever
cuando when
¿cuándo? when?
cuanto as much as; all that; **en —** as soon as

¿cuánto? how much? *pl.* how many?
cuarto *m.* room
cuatro four
Cuba *f.* Cuba
cubierto *p.p. of* cubrir
cubrir (*p.p.* **cubierto**) to cover
cuenta: darse — de to realize
cuidado *m.* care
cuidadosamente carefully
cuidar (**de**) to take care (of)
cultura *f.* culture
cumplir to fulfill, do
cuyo, –a whose, of which

CH

chico, –a small; *n.* boy (girl), young fellow
chino, –a Chinese

D

dar 4 to give; **—se cuenta de** to realize
de of, from
deber to owe; ought, must
deber *m.* duty
decidir to decide
decir 3 (*p.p.* **dicho**) to say, tell
dedicarse 6 (**a**) to devote oneself (to)
dejar to let, allow; to leave; **— de** (**hacer**) to stop (doing), fail to (do)
delante de in front of
delgado, –a slender
desaparecer 6 to disappear
descifrar to decipher
describir (*p.p.* **descrito**) to describe
descubrir (*p.p.* **descubierto**) to discover
desde from; since
desear to desire
despacio slowly
despacho *m.* office
despedir 5 (**i**) to dismiss; **—se de** to say goodbye to, take leave of
despertar 5 (**ie**) to awaken, wake up
después *adv.* afterwards, later; **— de** *prep.* after; **— (de) que** *conj.* after
destruir 7 to destroy
detener 3 to detain, arrest; **—se** to stop
devolver 5 to return (*something*)

día *m.* day; **todos los —s** every day
diablo *m.* devil
diciembre *m.* December
diente *m.* tooth
dificultad *f.* difficulty
dinero *m.* money
Dios *m.* God
dirección *f.* address
dirigir 6 to direct; **—se a** to address; to head for
disgusto *m.* annoyance, unpleasantness
disparate *m.* nonsense, absurdity
distinguido, –a distinguished
distinguir 6 to distinguish
divertido, –a amusing
divertir 5 (ie, i) to amuse, entertain; **—se** to have a good time
dólar *m.* dollar
doméstico, –a domestic
dominar to dominate
domingo *m.* Sunday
don Don (*title used before Christian names of men*)
donde where, in which
¿dónde? where?
doña Doña (*title used before Christian names of women*)
dormido, –a asleep, sleeping
dormir 5 (ue, u) to sleep; **—se** to fall asleep, go to sleep
dudar to doubt
dulce sweet; **—s** *m.* candy, sweets
durar to last
duro, –a hard

E

echar: **— a** to begin
edad *f.* age; **Edad Media** Middle Ages
edificio *m.* building
ejército *m.* army
el, los *def. art.* the
él *pers. pron.* he; (*after prep.*) him, it
elegante elegant
elegir 5 (i) to elect, choose
ella *pers. pron.* she; (*after prep.*) her, it
ellos, –as *pers. pron.* they; (*after prep.*) them
empezar 6 (ie) (a) to begin, start

emprender to undertake
en in, at, on
enamorado, –a in love
encaminarse a to head for, make one's way toward
encantador, –a charming
encantar to charm, delight
encender 5 (ie) to light, start (*a fire*)
encontrar 5 (ue) to find, come upon; **—se** to find oneself, be
enemigo *m.* enemy
enfadar to irritate, anger
enfermo, –a sick
enseñar to teach, show
ensimismado, –a lost in thought
entender 5 (ie) to understand
enterarse (de) to find out, inform oneself
entrar to enter, come in, go in
entregar to deliver, hand over, hand in
enviar 7 (í) to send
época *f.* epoch, period
escalera *f.* stairway, stairs
escapar to escape
escena *f.* scene
escoger 6 to choose, select
escribir (*p.p.* escrito) to write
escritor *m.* writer
escuela *f.* school
ese *dem. adj.* that; **ése** *dem. pron.* that (one)
eso *neut. dem. pron.* that
España *f.* Spain
español, –a *adj.* Spanish; *n.* Spaniard; *m.* Spanish (*language*)
esparcir 6 to scatter
especie *f.* species
esperar to hope; to wait (for)
esquina *f.* (outside) corner
estación *f.* station
Estados Unidos *m.* United States
estampido *m.* loud report (*as of a gun*)
estar 3 to be
este *dem. adj.* this; **éste** *dem. pron.* this (one)
esto *neut. dem. pron.* this
estrecho, –a narrow
estrella *f.* star

estudiante *m.* student
estudiar to study
examen *m.* examination
exigir 6 to demand, require
extranjero *m.* foreigner; **en el —** abroad
extrañar to surprise, cause wonder
extraño, –a strange

F

fabricante *m.* manufacturer
fácil easy
falta: hacer — to need, be needed
faltar to lack, be lacking; **le falta (dinero)** he lacks (money)
familia *f.* family
famoso, –a famous
fecha *f.* date
Felipe *m.* Philip
feliz happy
feria *f.* fair
fiar 7 (í) to trust
fiel faithful
fiero, –a fierce
fiesta *f.* holiday; party
fijarse (en) to notice
fila *f.* row
fin: a — de que in order that, so that
firmar to sign
flor *f.* flower
florecer 6 to blossom, flower, flourish
forzar 5 to force; to force open
francés, –a *adj.* French; *n.* Frenchman (Frenchwoman); *m.* French (*language*)
Francia *f.* France
frase *f.* phrase; sentence
fray Friar (*title used before Christian names in certain religious orders*)
frecuente frequent
fuente *f.* fountain
fuerte strong
fumar to smoke
función *f.* performance, show

G

gallina *f.* hen
ganancia *f.* profit, gain

ganar to win, earn
ganas: tener — de to feel like
gastar to spend (*money*)
gato *m.* cat
gaviota *f.* sea gull
general general
generoso, –a generous
genio *m.* genius
gobernar 5 to govern
gobierno *m.* government
gozar 6 (de) to enjoy
gracia *f.* grace; **hacer —** to amuse
graduarse 7 (ú) to graduate
gramática *f.* grammar
grande (gran) big, great
grave grave
grito *m.* cry, shout
guardar to keep; to guard
guerra *f.* war
guiar 7 (í) to guide
guitarra *f.* guitar
gustar to be pleasing; **le gusta (el libro)** he likes (the book)

H

Habana *f.* Havana
haber 3 to have (*auxiliary verb*)
hablador, –a talkative
hablar to speak, talk
hacer 3 (*p.p.* **hecho**) to do, make; **—se** to become
hacia toward
hasta to, as far as; until; **— que** *conj.* until
hay there is, there are; **— que** it is necessary to, one must
hecho *p.p.* of **hacer**
hermana *f.* sister
hermano *m.* brother
hermoso, –a beautiful
héroe *m.* hero
hierro *m.* iron
hijo *m.* son; *pl.* children
historia *f.* story, history
hola hello
holgazán, –a lazy
hombre *m.* man
hora *f.* hour, time

hoy today
huir 7 to flee, run away

I

idioma *m.* language
igualar to equal
impedir 5 (i) to prevent, hinder
importancia *f.* importance
importar to matter, be important
imposible impossible
impresión *f.* impression
inclinarse to bow
increíble unbelievable
indio, –a *adj. and n.* Indian
inferior inferior
infestar to infest
ingeniero *m.* engineer
inglés, –a *adj. and n.* English; *m.* English (*language*)
instante *m.* instant
insufrible insufferable
insulto *m.* insult
inteligencia *f.* intelligence
inteligente intelligent
interesante interesting
interesarse to be interested, become interested
interrumpir to interrupt
inventar to invent
invitar (a) to invite
ir 4 to go; **—se** to leave, go away
isla *f.* island
italiano, –a *adj. and n.* Italian; *m.* Italian (*language*)

J

jamás never, not . . . ever
Japón *m.* Japan
jardín *m.* garden
jefe *m.* chief, boss
Jorge George
José Joseph
joven *adj.* young; *n.* young man *or* woman
joya *f.* jewel
Juan John
juez *m.* judge

jugar 5 (**ue**) to play (*games*)
julio *m.* July
junio *m.* June
junto, –a joined; **—s** together
juventud *f.* youth

L

la *pers. pron.* her, it
la, las *def. art.* the
ladrillo *m.* brick
ladrón *m.* thief, robber
lago *m.* lake
lápiz *m.* pencil
largo, –a long
las *pers. pron.* them, you (*f.*)
lástima: ser — to be too bad, be a pity
Lazarillo de Tormes *16th-century Sp. picaresque novel*
le *pers. pron.* him; (to) him, her, you
lección *f.* lesson
leche *f.* milk
leer 7 to read
lejos far, distant; **a lo —** in the distance
lengua *f.* tongue; language
lentamente slowly
lento, –a slow
león *m.* lion
levantar to raise, lift; **—se** to rise, get up
ley *f.* law
libro *m.* book
limpiar to clean, wipe off
litro *m.* liter
lo *neut. def. art.* the; *pers. pron.* it
loco, –a crazy
locura *f.* insanity
lo que *rel. pron.* what
los *pers. pron.* them, you
luchar to struggle, fight
luego then, next
lunes *m.* Monday
luz *f.* light

LL

llamar to call, name; to knock (*at a door*); **se llama (Juan)** his name is (John)

llegar 6 to arrive
llevar to take, carry, wear
llorar to cry, weep
llover 5 (ue) to rain
lluvia *f.* rain

M

madre *f.* mother
madrileño, –a (person) from Madrid
magnífico, –a magnificent
maíz *m.* corn
mal *adv.* badly, ill
malo, –a bad; sick (*with* **estar**)
mamá *f.* mamma, mother
mandar to order, command; to send
manera *f.* manner; **de — que** so that
mano *f.* hand
manta *f.* blanket
manzana *f.* apple
mañana *f.* morning; *adv.* tomorrow
mapa *m.* map
marchar to march, walk; **—se** to leave
María Mary
marido *m.* husband
Marroquín, Francisco *16th-century Sp. bishop of Guatemala*
martes *m.* Tuesday
marzo *m.* March
más more; most; **— o menos** more or less
mayo *m.* May
mayor greater, greatest; older, oldest
me *pers. pron.* me, (to) me
médico *m.* doctor
medieval medieval
medio, –a half; **a las (ocho) y media** at half past (eight)
mejicano, –a Mexican
Méjico Mexico
mejor better, best
menor lesser, least
menos less, least; **a — que** unless
mentira *f.* lie; **parecer —** to be hard to believe
menudo: a — often
mercancía *f.* merchandise
mes *m.* month
mesa *f.* table; desk

meterse (en) to enter, slip into; to meddle
mi my
mí *prep. pron.* me
mientras (que) while
miércoles *m.* Wednesday
mil thousand
milla *f.* mile
millón *m.* million
mío, –a my, of mine
mirar to look, look at
mismo, –a self, very; same
misterioso, –a mysterious
mitad *f.* half
moderno, –a modern
modestia *f.* modesty
modo: de — que so that
molestar bother, annoy
momento *m.* moment
moral *f.* morality
morir 5 (ue, u) (*p.p.* **muerto**) to die; **—se** to die
mostrar 5 (ue) to show
mover 5 (ue) to move
muchacha *f.* girl, young woman
muchacho *m.* boy, young man
muchedumbre *f.* crowd
mucho, –a much, a lot; *pl.* many
mueble *m.* piece of furniture; **—s** furniture
muerte *f.* death
mujer *f.* woman; wife
mundo *m.* world; **todo el —** everybody
músico, –a musical
muy very

N

nación *f.* nation; **Naciones Unidas** United Nations
nada nothing, not . . . anything; *adv.* not . . . at all
nadar to swim
nadie nobody, no one, not . . . anyone
naipe *m.* playing card
naranja *f.* orange
Navidades *f.* Christmas (season)
necesario, –a necessary
necesitar to need

negar 5 (ie) to deny; —se (a) to refuse
negocio *m.* business
negro, –a black
neolítico, –a Neolithic
ni neither, nor; — ... — neither ...
nor
ninguno, –a *indef. adj. and pron.* no,
not ... any, none
niña *f.* child
niño *m.* child
no no, not
noche *f.* night
nos *pers. pron.* us, (to) us
nosotros, –as *pers. pron.* we; *(after
prep.)* us
novelista *m. and f.* novelist
novia *f.* "girl," sweetheart, bride
novio *m.* "boy friend," fiancé, groom
nuestro, –a our, of ours
nueve nine
nuevo, –a new
número *m.* number
nunca never, not ... ever

O

obispo *m.* bishop
obscuro, –a dark
ocurrir to occur, happen
ocho eight
oficial *m.* officer
ofrecer 6 to offer
oír 4 to hear
¡ojalá! would that! (I wish that)
ojo *m.* eye
oler 5 (hue) to smell
olvidarse (de) to forget
once eleven
opinión *f.* opinion
optimista *m. and f.* optimist
ordenar to order, command
origen *m.* origin
orilla *f.* bank, shore
Orizaba *mountain peak in Mexico*
oro *m.* gold
os *pers. pron.* you *(fam. pl.)*, (to) you
otoño *m.* autumn, fall
otro, –a other, another
oveja *f.* sheep

P

Pablo Paul
padre *m.* father
pagar 6 to pay
página *f.* page
pájaro *m.* bird
palacio *m.* palace
pálido, –a pale
pañuelo *m.* handkerchief
papá *m.* papa
papel *m.* paper
paquete *m.* package
par *m.* couple, pair
para for, in order to, by; — que in order
that, so that
paraguas *m.* umbrella
paraje *m.* place
parecer 6 to seem, appear; — mentira
to be hard to believe; —se (a) to
resemble
París *m.* Paris
parte *f.* part; en todas —s everywhere
partido *m.* game, match
partir to depart; to divide
pasado, –a past, last
pasar to pass, spend *(time)*; to happen
pasear(se) to stroll, walk
pastor *m.* shepherd
patria *f.* fatherland, homeland
paz *f.* peace
pedir 5 (i) to ask, ask for
Pedro Peter
película *f.* film
peligro *m.* danger
pelo *m.* hair
penicilina *f.* penicillin
pensar 5 (ie) to think; — + *inf.* to
intend
peor worse, worst
Pepe Joe
pequeño, –a little, small
perder 5 (ie) to lose
periódico *m.* newspaper
permitir to permit
perro *m.* dog
perseguir 6 (i) to pursue
Perú *m.* Peru
peruano, –a Peruvian

pesado, -a heavy; boring
petición *f.* petition
piano *m.* piano
pícaro *m.* rogue, rascal
pico *m.* peak
pintar to paint
pintor *m.* painter
playa *f.* beach
pluma *f.* feather; pen
pobre poor
poco, -a little, few; *adv.* little; **por —** almost, nearly
poder 3 (ue) to be able, can, could
poder *m.* power
poema *m.* poem
poeta *m.* poet
poetisa *f.* poetess
policía *m.* policeman
política *f.* politics
político *m.* politician
pólvora *f.* (gun) powder
poner 3 (*p.p.* **puesto**) to put, place; **—se** to become; **—se a** to begin, start
por by, for, through, along
portarse to behave
portero *m.* doorman
poseer 7 to possess, own
posible possible
precio *m.* price
preciso necessary
preferir 5 (ie, i) to prefer
preguntar to ask (*a question*)
preguntón, -a inquisitive
premio *m.* prize
presentarse to appear, show up
presidente *m.* president
preso, -a seized by
prestar to lend
prima *f.* cousin
primero, -a first
prisa *f.* haste; **de —** fast
problema *m.* problem
producir 6 to produce
profesor *m.* professor
profundamente profoundly, deeply
pronto soon; **de —** suddenly
proyecto *m.* project
pueblo *m.* town

puerta *f.* door
pues then; well
puesto *m.* job, position
puntual punctual
punto *m.* point; **en —** sharp (*of time*)

Q

que *rel. pron.* who, whom, that, which; **el —, la —** he who, she who, the one who; **lo —** what; **—** (*after a comparative*) than
¿ qué ? what ? which ? **¿ qué tal ?** how ? how goes it ?
quedar to remain, be left behind; **—se** to remain, stay behind
quejarse (de) to complain (about)
quemar to burn, tan (*by the sun*)
querer 3 (ie) to wish, want, love (*a person*)
quien *rel. pron.* who, he who, anyone who; **a —** whom
¿ quién ? who ? **¿ a quién ?** whom ? **¿ de quién ?** whose ?
quinto, -a fifth
quitar to take away, take off; **—se** to take off (*clothes*)
quizás perhaps

R

rápidamente rapidly
rápido, -a rapid
raza *f.* race
realizar 6 to fulfill, carry out, realize
recibir to receive
recoger 6 to pick up, gather
recordar 5 (ue) to remember, recall
redondo, -a round
referirse 5 (ie, i) **a** to refer to
regalo *m.* present, gift
región *f.* region
regla *f.* rule
reír 5 (i) to laugh; **—se (de)** to laugh (at)
religión *f.* religion
reloj *m.* clock, watch
remoto, -a remote
reñir 5 (i) to scold, quarrel
repetir 5 (i) to repeat

república *f.* republic
responder to reply
respuesta *f.* reply
resultado *m.* result
retirarse to retire
retumbar to sound loudly
revés *m.* reverse
rey *m.* king
rico, –a rich
robar to rob, steal
rodear to surround
rogar 6 (ue) to request, ask
rojo, –a red
romper (*p.p.* roto) to break, tear
rubí *m.* ruby
rubio, –a blond
ruido *m.* noise
ruso, –a *adj. and n.* Russian; *m.* Russian (*language*)

S

sábado *m.* Saturday
saber 3 to know, find out
sacar 6 to take out, extract
sacrificar 6 to sacrifice
sal *f.* salt
sala *f.* living room
salir 4 to go out, come out, leave; — bien to succeed, pass (*an examination*)
salud *f.* health
saludar to greet
santo, –a holy, sainted; *n.* saint
se *refl. pron.* himself, herself, (to) himself, *etc.*
seco, –a dry
secretaria *f.* secretary
seis six
seguida: en — at once, immediately
seguir 6 (i) to follow, continue
semana *f.* week
senador *m.* senator
senda *f.* path
sentado, –a sitting
sentar 5 (ie) to seat; —se to sit down
sentido *m.* sense
sentir 5 (ie, i) to feel, regret; —se + adj. or p.p. to feel (*sad, sick, etc.*)
seña *f.* sign

señor *m.* gentleman, Mr.
señora *f.* lady, wife, Mrs.
señorita *f.* young lady, Miss
separar to separate
ser 4 to be
sereno, –a serene, calm
serie *f.* series
servir 5 (i) to serve
Sevilla *f.* Seville
si if
sí yes
sí *refl. prep. pron.* himself, herself, yourself, yourselves, themselves
siempre always
siglo *m.* century
siguiente following
silla *f.* chair, saddle
simpático, –a likeable, appealing, nice
sin *prep.* without; — que *conj.* without
sino (*used after negatives*) but
sistema *m.* system
sobrino *m.* nephew
socialista *m. and f.* socialist
sofá *m.* sofa
sol *m.* sun
soldado *m.* soldier
soler 5 (ue) to be in the habit of, used to + *inf.*
solitario, –a solitary
sombrero *m.* hat
soñar 5 (ue) (con) to dream (about)
sopa *f.* soup
sor Sister (*title used before Christian names in certain religious orders*)
su his, her, your, their
subir to climb, go up
suceder to happen
suelo *m.* ground, floor
suerte *f.* luck
sufrido, –a long-suffering
suizo, –a Swiss
superior superior
supuesto que supposing that
suyo, –a his, of his; hers, of hers; *etc.*

T

tal such, such a; — vez perhaps; con — (de) que provided

tampoco neither, not . . . either
tan so, as
tanto, −a so much, as much; *pl.* so
  many, as many; — . . . como as
  much (many) . . . as
tardar (en) to delay, be long in
tarde *f.* afternoon
tarea *f.* task
taza *f.* cup
te *pers. pron.* you (*fam.*); (to) you
teléfono *m.* telephone
tema *m.* theme
temer to fear
temor *m.* fear
temprano *adv.* early
tendencia *f.* tendency
tener 3 to have; — ganas de to feel
  like; — que to have to
tenis *m.* tennis
tercero, −a third
terminar to end, finish
tesis *f.* thesis
ti *prep. pron.* you (*fam.*)
tía *f.* aunt
tiempo *m.* time, weather; hacer buen
  (mal) — to be good (bad) weather
tierra *f.* earth, land
tigre *m.* tiger
tío *m.* uncle
tocar 6 to play (*a musical instru-
  ment*)
todo, −a all, whole
Tomás Thomas
tontería *f.* nonsense, piece of nonsense
tormentoso, −a stormy
torpe dull, stupid
torre *f.* tower
tortuoso, −a winding
trabajar to work
trabajo *m.* work
traer 4 to bring
traje *m.* suit
trasero, −a back, rear
tratar de to try; —se de to be a question of
treinta thirty
tren *m.* train
tres three
triste sad

trueno *m.* thunder clap; —s thunder
tu your (*fam.*)
tú *pers. pron.* you (*fam.*)
tumba *f.* tomb
tuyo, −a your, of yours (*fam.*)

U

último, −a last
universidad *f.* university
un(o), una (*indef. art. and numeral*) a,
  an, one; *pl.* some, a few, a pair
usted, −es *pers. pron.* you

V

vaca *f.* cow
vago, −a vague
valer 4 to be worth
valle *m.* valley
vanidad *f.* vanity
variar 7 (í) to vary
vaso *m.* (drinking) glass
vecino *m.* neighbor
veinte twenty
vencer 6 to conquer, overcome
vender to sell
venir 3 to come
ventana *f.* window
ver 4 (*p.p.* visto) to see
verano *m.* summer
verdad *f.* truth
vestir 5 (i) to dress; —se to get dressed
vez *f.* time (occasion); alguna — ever;
  otra — again; repetidas veces often,
  repeatedly; tal — perhaps
viaje *m.* trip, voyage
vida *f.* life
viejo, −a old
viernes *m.* Friday
virgen *f.* virgin
virtud *f.* virtue
visitar to visit
vivo, −a alive, lively
voluntad *f.* will (power)
volver 5 (ue) (*p.p.* vuelto) to return,
  come back; —se to turn around;
  —se loco to go crazy
vosotros, −as *pers. pron.* you (*fam. pl.*)
vuestro, −a your, of yours (*fam. pl.*)

Y

y and
ya already, now, presently
yo *pers. pron.* I

Z

zapato *m.* shoe
zoología *f.* zoology

English-Spanish Vocabulary

In this vocabulary the chapter treating each irregular verb is indicated by printing the number of the chapter after the infinitive: **andar** 3.

A

a, an *indef. art.* un, una
able: be able poder 3 (ue)
about (*before numbers*) unos, –as
accept aceptar
accompany acompañar
act (**behave**) portarse
actress actriz *f.*
advantage: take — of aprovecharse de
advice consejo *m.* (*Use pl. unless only one piece of advice is meant.*)
advisable: be — convenir 3
advise aconsejar
affair asunto *m.*
afraid: be — temer, tener 3 miedo
after *adv.* después; *prep.* después de; *conj.* después (de) que
afternoon tarde *f.*
airplane avión *m.*, aeroplano *m.*
airport aeropuerto *m.*
already ya
always siempre
all todo, –a; **not ... at —** nada
American americano, –a
amusing divertido, –a
and y
another otro, –a
anybody alguien; **not ... —** nadie
anyone alguien; **not ... —** nadie
anything: not ... — nada
appear (**show up**) presentarse
applaud aplaudir
April abril *m.*
arrive llegar 6
artist artista *m. and f.*
artistic artístico, –a
as como; **— ... —** tan ... como
ascertain averiguar 6
ask (*a question*) preguntar; **— for** pedir 5 (i)
at en, a
attend asistir (a)

B

back: be — estar de vuelta; **come —** volver 5
bank (*river*) orilla *f.*
Barcelona Barcelona *f.*
battle batalla *f.*
be ser 4, estar 3
beautiful hermoso, –a; bello, –a
become (**look well on**) sentar 5 bien a
bed cama *f.*; **go to —** acostarse 5 (ue)
before *adv.* antes; *prep.* antes de; *conj.* antes (de) que
believe creer 7
belong to ser de
best mejor
better mejor
bird pájaro *m.*
black-haired de pelo negro
boat barco *m.*
book libro *m.*
boss patrón *m.*, jefe *m.*
both los (las) dos; ambos, –as
boy muchacho *m.*
branch rama *f.*
Brazil El Brasil *m.*
bread pan *m.*
break romper (*p.p.* roto)
breakfast desayuno *m.*
bridge puente *m.*
bring traer 4
brother hermano *m.*; **brother(s) and sister(s)** hermanos
bullfighter torero *m.*
but pero; (*after neg.*) sino
buy comprar

C

café café *m.*
call llamar
can poder 3 (ue)
Canyon: The Grand — El Gran Canyón

captain capitán *m.*
car automóvil *m.*, coche *m.*
career carrera *f.*
catch coger 6
Catholic católico, –a
celebrated célebre
cello violoncelo *m.*
chair silla *f.*
chapter capítulo *m.*
child niño *m.*, niña *f.*
cigarette cigarrillo *m.*
class clase *f.*
climb subir
close cerrar 5 (ie)
coffee café *m.*
cold frío, –a; **to be —** (*weather*) hacer 3 frío
cold resfriado *m.*
Columbus Colón
come venir 4; **— for** venir por; **— out** salir 4
comedy comedia *f.*
comfortable cómodo, –a
complain (of) quejarse (de)
conduct conducir 4
conquer vencer 6
consent (to) consentir 5 (ie, i) (en)
continue continuar 7 (ú)
cook *v.* cocinar; *n.* cocinera *f.*
count contar 5 (ue)
country país *m.*
cousin primo *m.*
cover cubrir (*p.p.* cubierto)
cross cruzar 6
cry llorar
Cuba Cuba *f.*
Cuban cubano, –a
cup taza *f.*
cure curar

D

dance baile *m.*
date fecha *f.*
day día *m.*; **all —** todo el día; **every —** todos los días
December diciembre *m.*
decide decidir
demand exigir 6

deny negar 6 (ie)
depart partir
deserve merecer 6
destroy destruir 7
die morir 5 (*p.p.* muerto)
difficult difícil
dinner comida *f.*
direct dirigir 6
disappear desaparecer 6
discover descubrir (*p.p.* descubierto)
dismiss despedir 5 (i)
distinguish distinguir 6
do hacer 3 (*p.p.* hecho)
doctor médico *m.*
dog perro *m.*
dollar dólar *m.*
Dominic Domingo
Don don
Don Quixote Don Quijote
door puerta *f.*
dress: get dressed vestirse 5 (i)
drink beber

E

each cada; **— other** nos, os, se
early temprano
earn ganar
eat comer
effortlessly sin esfuerzo
empire imperio *m.*
employment empleo *m.*
enough bastante
Europe Europa *f.*
even: — though aunque
ever jamás, alguna vez; **not... —** nunca
every todos los (todas las) ...
everybody todo el mundo
everywhere en (por) todas partes

F

fail dejar (de)
fall caer 4
famous famoso, –a
fan (devotee) aficionado *m.*
father padre *m.*
fear temer
find encontrar 5, hallar

fire (dismiss) despedir 5
first primero, –a
fish pescar 6
fit caber 3
flee huir 7
flower flor *f.*
fly volar 5
follow seguir 6 (i)
fond of aficionado, (–a) a
fool tonto *m.*
for para, por
forget olvidar
four hundred cuatrocientos, –as
Frenchman francés *m.*
frequently frecuentemente, con frecuencia
fresh fresco, –a
friend amigo *m.*, amiga *f.*
from de

G

garden jardín *m.*
get (receive) tener 3; How do you — to...? ¿ Cómo se va a ...? — to (reach) llegar 6 a
girl muchacha *f.*; — friend novia *f.*
give dar 4
glass (*for drinking*) vaso *m.*
go ir 4; — away irse; — to bed acostarse 5 (ue)
gold oro *m.*
good bueno, –a
Granada Granada *f.*
grateful agradecido, –a
great grande (gran)
greet saludar
guest huésped *m.*, invitado *m.*
guide guiar 7 (í)

H

ham jamón *m.*
hand mano *f.*
happen pasar, suceder
happy feliz
hard *adv.* mucho; be — to believe parecer mentira
hat sombrero *m.*

Havana La Habana *f.*
have tener 3; (*auxiliary*) haber 3; to — to tener que
he él
hear oír 4
help ayudar
her *pers. pron.* (*dir. obj.*) la; (*indir. obj.*) le; (*after prep.*) ella
here aquí
heroic heroico, –a
him *pers. pron.* (*dir. obj.*) le, lo; (*indir. obj.*) le; (*after prep.*) él
himself *subject* él mismo; (*after prep.*) sí mismo
his su
home casa *f.*, hogar; at — en casa; (*toward*) — a casa
homely feo, –a
hope esperar
horse caballo *m.*
hospital hospital *m.*
hotel hotel *m.*
house casa *f.*
how? ¿ cómo ?
huge enorme

I

I yo
if si
important importante
impossible imposible
in en
influence influencia *f.*
intelligent inteligente
interest interesar
it *pers. pron.* (*dir. obj.*) lo, la
Italian *adj.* italiano, –a

J

John Juan
June junio *m.*
just: have — acabar de

K

keep guardar
key llave *f.*

king rey *m.*; **the — and queen** los reyes
knock (at the door) llamar (a la puerta)
know (*knowledge*) saber 3; **— how**
　saber; (*acquaintance*) conocer 6

L

large grande
last (*in a series*) último, –a; (*passed*)
　pasado, –a
last durar
later más tarde, después
laugh reír 5 (i)
law derecho *m.*; ley *f.*
lawyer abogado *m.*
leaf hoja *f.*
learn aprender
learned sabio, –a
leave irse 4, marcharse, salir 4 (de)
lend prestar
lesson lección *f.*
let (allow) dejar; **— (have)** que + *3rd*
　pers. pres. subjunctive
letter carta *f.*
library biblioteca *f.*
life vida *f.*
lift levantar
like *prep.* como
like *v.* gustar; **he likes (the book)** le
　gusta (el libro)
live vivir
living *n.* vivir *m.*
London Londres *m.*
long largo, –a; **— live!** ¡ viva !
look mirar; **— at** mirar; **— for** buscar 6
lose perder 5 (ie)
love: in — enamorado, –a

M

Madrid Madrid *m.*
maid criada *f.*
mailman cartero *m.*
make hacer 3 (*p.p.* hecho)
man hombre *m.*
many muchos, –as
Mary María
matter: no — how por + *adj. or adv.*
　+ *subjunctive*

me *pers. pron.* me
mean querer 3 decir 3
meet (encounter) encontrar 5 (ue);
　(*become acquainted with*) conocer 6
Mexican mejicano, –a
Mexico Méjico *m.* (*or* México)
milk leche *f.*
mine *adj.* mío, –a
modern moderno, –a
moment momento *m.*
money dinero *m.*
more más
morning mañana *f.*
most más
mother madre *f.*
movies cine *m.*
Mr. señor *m.*, Sr.
Mrs. señora *f.*, Sra.
much mucho, –a; *adv.* mucho
music música *f.*

N

name nombre *m.*; **family —** apellido *m.*
necktie corbata *f.*
need necesitar
never nunca
new nuevo, –a
newspaper periódico *m.*
New York Nueva York *f.*
next siguiente, próximo, que viene
nineteenth diez y nueve
nobody nadie
noon mediodía *m.*; **at —** a mediodía
notice advertir 5 (ie, i)
notify avisar
novel novela *f.*
now ahora, ya

O

obey obedecer 6
o'clock la, las + *cardinal number;* la
　una, las dos, *etc.*
of de
offer ofrecer 6
often a menudo
old viejo, –a; **be ... years —** tener
　... años

on en; — **Saturdays** los sábados
once una vez; **at** — en siguida
one uno, un, una; **the** — **who, which**
  el que, la que, *etc.*
open abrir (*p.p.* abierto)
other otro, –a
our nuestro, –a
overtake alcanzar 6
own poseer 7

P

paint pintar
pair unos, –as
paper papel *m.*; **news**— periódico
parents padres *m.*
park parque *m.*
Paris París *m.*
part: the best — ... lo mejor ...
past pasado *m.*
patiently pacientemente
patio patio *m.*
Paul Pablo
pay pagar 6
pen pluma *f.*
perhaps acaso, quizás, tal vez
permit permitir
person persona *f.*
pick up recoger 6
picture cuadro *m.*
place poner 3 (*p.p.* puesto)
play (*games*) jugar a 5; (*musical instru-
  ments*) tocar 6
pleasant agradable
poor pobre
post office correo *m.*
pound libra *f.*
power poder *m.*
powerful poderoso, –a
prepare preparar
present presente; **at** — actualmente
presently (**soon**) ya
president presidente *m.*
pretty bonito, –a
Prime Minister Primer Ministro *m.*
problem problema *m.*
produce producir 6
professor profesor *m.*
progressive progresivo, –a
protest protestar

provided con tal (de) que
put poner 3 (*p.p.* puesto); — **out**
  apagar 6

Q

quickly aprisa, rápidamente

R

read leer 7
ready listo, –a; preparado, –a
realize darse cuenta (de)
receive recibir
refuse negarse 6 (ie) (a); **no querer** 3
regret sentir 5 (ie, i)
remember recordar 5
rent alquilar
reply responder
resemble parecerse 6 (a)
return volver 5 (*p.p.* vuelto)
rich rico, –a
right: be — tener 3 razón
river río *m.*
road camino *m.*
Roman romano, –a
room cuarto *m.*; **living** — sala *f.*
rule regla *f.*
run correr
Russian *adj. and n.* ruso, –a; — **language** ruso *m.*

S

saddle silla *f.*
saint santo, –a
same mismo, –a
Saturday *m.* sábado
save ahorrar
say decir 3 (*p.p.* dicho)
scatter esparcir 6
school escuela *f.*
seat sentar 5 (ie)
secretary secretario *m.*, secretaria *f.*
see ver 2 (*p.p.* visto)
seek buscar 6
Seine Sena *m.*
seize coger 6
sell vender
senator senador *m.*
send enviar 7 (í)
servant criado *m.*, criada *f.*

serve servir 5 (i)
seven siete
seven hundred setecientos, –as
seventy-one setenta y uno, –a
she ella
shoe zapato *m.*
shout *v.* gritar; *n.* grito *m.*
show mostrar 5 (ue), enseñar
sick malo, –a; enfermo, –a
Sierra Nevada Sierra Nevada *f.*
sign firmar
since desde
singing cantar *m.*
sister hermana *f.*
sister-in-law cuñada *f.*
sit (down) sentarse 5 (ie)
sitting *adj.* sentado, –a
sleep dormir 5 (ue, u)
sleeping *adj.* dormido, –a
slowly lentamente, despacio
smell oler 5 (hue)
snow nieve *f.*
so: — **that** para que; de modo que
solve resolver 5 (ue)
solved resuelto, –a (*p.p. of* resolver)
some alguno, –a
somebody alguien
someone alguien
somewhat *adv.* algo
son hijo *m.*
soon pronto; **as — as** en cuanto; **as —
  as possible** lo más pronto posible
sound (noise) ruido *m.*
Spain España *f.*
Spaniard español *m.*, española *f.*
Spanish *adj.* español, –a; — **language**
  español *m.*
speak hablar
spend (*time*) pasar
spite: in — of a pesar de
stairs escalera *f.*
strong fuerte
student estudiante *m.*, alumno *m.*,
  alumna *f.*
study estudiar
such tal; — **a** tal
suit traje *m.*
suppose: Who do you suppose he was?
  ¿ Quién sería ?

surrounded (by) rodeado, –a (de)
swim nadar

T

take tomar; llevar; — **advantage of**
  aprovecharse de; — **off** quitarse; —
  out sacar 6; — **part** tomar parte
talk hablar
taste estar 3 (*See Chapter 18.*)
team equipo *m.*
telegram telegrama *m.*
ten diez
tennis tenis *m.*
than que
that *dem. adj.* ese, aquel; *neut. dem.
  pron.* eso
that *rel. pron. and conj.* que
the *def. art.* el, la, los, las
their su
them *pers. pron.* los, las; **(to) them** les;
  (*after prep.*) ellos, ellas
there ahí, allí, allá; — **is (are)** hay
thing cosa *f.*
third tercero, –a
this *dem. adj.* este; *neut. dem. pron.*
  esto
though: even — aunque
three tres
Thursday jueves *m.*
time tiempo *m.*; **have a good —** divertirse 5 (ie, i); **it is — to** es hora de;
  on — a tiempo
to a
Toledo Toledo *m.*
tourist turista *m. and f.*
town pueblo *m.*
tree árbol *m.*
trip viaje *m.*
truck camión *m.*
try tratar de
twenty veinte
twice dos veces
two dos
two hundred doscientos, –as

U

unable: be — no poder 3 (ue)
uncle tío *m.*

understand entender 5 (ie), comprender

university universidad *f.*; *adj.* universitario, –a

us *pers. pron.* nos; (*after prep.*) nosotros, –as

used to soler 5 (ue); *imperfect tense; for example,* he used to study estudiaba

usual *adv.* de costumbre

V

vary variar 7 (í)

very muy

vote votar (por)

W

wait (for) esperar

wake up despertar 5 (ie)

walk andar 3

wallet cartera *f.*

want querer 3

watch reloj *m.*

we nosotros, –as

weapon arma *f.*

week semana *f.*

well bien

what *rel. pron.* lo que; —**ever** lo que + *subjunctive*

what? ¿qué? ¿cuál? ¿cómo? (*See Chapter 20: A, II, III, IV.*); — **a!** ¡qué!

when cuando

where donde

where? ¿dónde?

which que

which? ¿cuál?

while mientras (que)

white blanco, –a

who que

who? ¿quién?

whom? ¿a quién? (*or* quién *with whatever prep. the sense requires*)

whose? ¿de quién?

why? ¿por qué? **why!** ¡si...!

wife esposa *f.*, mujer *f.*

wish querer 3; I —! ¡ojalá!

with con; — me conmigo

without *prep.* sin; *conj.* sin que

woman mujer *f.*

word palabra *f.*

work trabajar

world mundo *m.*; **New** — **Nuevo Mundo**

worth: be worth valer 4

write escribir (*p.p.* escrito)

writer escritor *m.*

Y

year año *m.*

yesterday ayer

you *subject pron.* tú (*fam.*), usted, –es

young joven

youngest menor

your tu (*fam.*), su (*formal*)

Index

Index